Hele[illegible] [illegible]th
Shan[illegible]ghai - 1933

50

CRY HAVOC!

Other books by

BEVERLEY NICHOLS

EVENSONG
CRAZY PAVEMENTS
PRELUDE
PATCHWORK
SELF
TWENTY-FIVE
THE STAR SPANGLED MANNER
ARE THEY THE SAME AT HOME?
WOMEN AND CHILDREN LAST
DOWN THE GARDEN PATH
FOR ADULTS ONLY
FAILURES

CRY HAVOC!

by

BEVERLEY NICHOLS

'Cry Havoc, and let slip
the dogs of war'

JONATHAN CAPE
THIRTY BEDFORD SQUARE LONDON

FIRST PUBLISHED 1933
SECOND IMPRESSION, JULY, 1933
THIRD IMPRESSION, AUGUST, 1933

JONATHAN CAPE LTD. 30 BEDFORD SQUARE, LONDON
AND 91 WELLINGTON STREET WEST, TORONTO

PRINTED IN GREAT BRITAIN IN THE CITY OF OXFORD
AT THE ALDEN PRESS
PAPER MADE BY JOHN DICKINSON & CO., LTD.
BOUND BY A. W. BAIN & CO., LTD.

CONTENTS

To

THOSE MOTHERS WHOSE SONS ARE STILL ALIVE

CRY HAVOC!

CHAPTER I

DEAR H. G. WELLS . . .

Dear H. G. Wells,

You may remember that some months ago we found ourselves walking together down one of those little streets that huddle together, like poor relations, in the proud shadow of Mayfair. It was an afternoon in late spring — one of those quiet and exquisite London afternoons which cannot decide whether to dress in gold or in silver . . . for all the roofs were gold, but the plumes of smoke which trembled over the chimneys were palest silver, and so were the cobbled pavements, where the light caught them.

We had been lunching with a charming lady in surroundings which were a little strange to both of us — for Punch's club — I think that was its name — was certainly the queerest background against which I ever hope to see you. There you were, sitting on a high stool against a cocktail bar, sipping water and nibbling hot hors d'œuvres, and occasionally paying a charmingly phrased compliment to one of the slim and geranium-lipped girls who made up our party. I could not decide whether you liked the party or hated it . . . I only knew that I was hating it. For the neurosis which now haunts me, with increasing dread, was just beginning in those days. And I was impatient of Punch's club, and the people in it, and all that they stood for. I wanted to get out into the fresh air and talk to you . . . about the next war, whose echo then seemed near enough, though it has grown alarmingly nearer, in the meantime.

We did talk, at last, and when you heard that I had managed to persuade a highly respectable magazine to accept a fiery article which was called 'In the Next War I Shall Be a Conscientious Objector', you told me that I should probably get into trouble now, though I should be 'laying up treasure for myself in the future'.

I have often wondered what you meant by that phrase. I feel sure that you did *not* mean that the article would prove comforting evidence to produce at the military tribunal before which, presumably, I shall be called. Because the article, in itself, is a form of death-warrant in that I publicly proclaim in it my desire to be shot in the nearest backyard, within twenty-four hours of the declaration of war, rather than shoot, or gas, or drown, or otherwise murder any of my fellow men. If a man makes that statement and means it, and if he makes it often enough, and if he is not entirely unknown by the public, it is presumed that he will either have to stand by it, when the hour comes, or else be denounced as such a hypocrite and a coward that life will be unendurable for him.

I am still prepared to stand by it, but I am no longer sure that I shall be called upon to do so, because my individual problem, in the face of war, no longer seems so simple that it can be solved by conscientious objection. In other words my pacifism is no longer passivism. That is what a little honest research does for a man! And since you are really the cause of all the trouble, perhaps I may remind you of your own words, which have been ringing in my memory like a maddening peal of bells.

'*War is no more to be ended by saying, "No more war" and "I stand out," and declaring that every government that went into the Great War was just as bad as any other and indeed on the whole worse, than is burglary to be ended by speaking in tones of remonstrance to a policeman who uses his truncheon.*

'*The absolute pacifists' refusal of service is not therefore so much an action against their own state as an incantation to the unknown, unimplemented God of Peace. In that god they put their faith — and so, gesticulating sceptical disapproval and moral superiority towards all who seek to grapple with Mars in his panoply, towards all who subjugate chaotic by ordered force, they liberate their minds to ease and agreeable occupations. Other people will do the dusty and laborious job, and then, if these others succeed, will they not be justified in their faith in that unknown power?*'

II

Of course it is inevitable that sooner or later any honest pacifist must bring himself to face this accusation, even if it is not you who brings it to his notice. The very glibness and facility of the pure non-resistance argument is enough to make it suspect. Indeed, at the outset of my little non-resistance campaign, which took me before all manner of audiences, from Whitechapel to the slums of Berlin, I was made a little doubtful by the ease with which audiences of every type could be induced to cheer statements of extreme pacifism. There was, for example, an occasion when, at the Albert Hall, I declared, before an audience of ten thousand people, that 'just as the mother of a drunkard's children ought to thank God if her sons grew up to take the pledge so ought the mother of a soldier's children to thank God if her sons grew up to be conscientious objectors.' The storm of cheers which greeted this somewhat sweeping statement was as gratifying as it was unexpected — but, in retrospect, the episode seemed a little less satisfactory. Were cheers of this sort really significant? Were they not dangerously similar to the sort of cheers which rang out in 1918, when eminent Englishmen in every walk of life rose to their feet and informed audiences that Germany must 'pay for the war to the last penny' — a statement so lunatic that one blinks when one comes across it, as one frequently does, in the newspapers of that distant period?

Mind you, I am not trying to back out of the extreme pacifist attitude of complete non-resistance. It *may* be right, after all . . . I shall not have made up my mind until I have written this book, which is the reason why I am writing it. I merely want to see what happens when a man faces the facts. And to whatever conclusion I may be led, it is necessary to reiterate the fact that by temperament, by instinct, by whatever word you may choose for the bundle of mysterious, inherited, chemical reactions which go to make a man's soul, I am a pacifist of the pacifists. I believe, for example, that the discussion of war should *begin* with the personal agony of the soldier and should *end* with the political and economic frictions which result in that agony. In the same way I think that the discussion of poverty should *begin* with the realization of empty stomachs and squalid rooms and should *end* with statistics. If that sounds involved, I would merely explain, humbly, that I am trying to say that I should like to see a model of a hideously wounded soldier on the respectable tables of disarmament conferences, and I should like all parliamentary debates on unemployment relief to be carried out in the sombre and fœtid atmosphere of a Glasgow slum. . . .

III

None the less, it is useless to attack this hydra-headed monster of war in a state of wild and unreasoning emotion. As you yourself have stated, that is what the average pacifist does. He rails against the 'horrors of war', and having railed, shrugs his shoulders and says that he will have none of the nasty business. This is not really a very helpful attitude to the average man, though it may be and often is, a noble one. The trouble about it is that it ignores the fact that man is a social animal and is unable to stand aside on matters of national policy.

An out-and-out pacifist, to be absolutely logical, would have to deduct from his income-tax that proportion of it which would be spent on armaments, and would have to withhold this sum, even at the cost of suffering imprisonment. An out-and-out pacifist is therefore, *ipso facto*, an anarchist. It may be that he is right to be an anarchist — it may be that this denial of systems is the one system which would work. That is not the point. The point is that you cannot be an anarchist on some things and a constitutional liberal on others.

I began writing this book in the true anarchical, peace-at-any-price spirit. But I soon had to stop. It was not only your influence which made me tear up so many sheets of manuscript. It was the inevitable logic of outside events. For though I wanted to carry my pacific banner through every crowd which I might encounter, the state of Europe made me wonder if I should even be able to get it through the customs at Dover. Before I had written a dozen pages, I had to lay down my pen, and thus apostrophize myself:

'I am fighting in a world whose skies are slashed and tormented by the banners of discordant nationalities. I want to tear down those banners – the reds and the blues and the yellows – because they are shutting out the sun. I want to follow the white flag of peace only. But can I? In a world where Germany is a sullen, straining giant, rattling at the prison bars, where France, like a nervous gaoler, struts down the corridors of Europe, jangling her keys in her pocket, where the whole Italian population is being turned into an army, drilled with operatic precision, and where the Russian limelight bathes both East and West in a strange glow that has never yet been seen on land or sea?

'Where does the white flag of peace lead a man, through such lands? Can I keep it flying through Spain, for example, who has celebrated her entry into the revolutionary brotherhood of nations by plastering her coast with titanic guns? Or through Rumania, whose musical-comedy officers have their highly manicured hands tight round the nation's throat? Or through Greece and Turkey, whose snarlings make a hell of the whole Near East?

'And what will happen when I try to carry it to the Far East? Will it be torn from my hands and trampled in the mud of some Japanese ditch? And if I wave it on the Indian frontier how will it appeal to the Afridis, if they take it into their heads to raid Peshawar? And what will be the response to it of the great democracy of America?'

Such questions made me realize that this book was going to be difficult to write. How difficult, at that time, I had not the faintest idea. If you do me the honour of reading it you will be the first to recognize that it is not a book at all – it is only a series of agonized plunges into a forest of problems which bristles with poisoned thorns. The forest is so deep, the thorns so sharp, that constantly I have longed for the keen sword of your intellect, if only for an hour, that I might slash through the undergrowth and see the light. But I had to struggle on by myself. And though the result may be pitiable, though I may only have made a gap, here and there, where you would have cut a clear path, perhaps the very feebleness of my efforts will encourage some others to better them.

I was considerably helped, in tackling the problem, by borrowing the device which you used in your *Wealth, Work and Happiness of Mankind*, i.e. the supposition of an imaginary museum containing all the data which you desired, but found to be unavailable. To compare these few and scattered essays with a work such as yours would be an impudence of which I could not be guilty, even in jest. But for the benefit of the reader it may be stated that the only way in which it seemed possible for a writer of average intelligence to make up his mind on his personal attitude to this question of war and peace was by asking himself what would be the *perfect* book to write about it. And having asked myself this question I eventually came to the conclusion that the perfect book would be divided into four parts, in which the writer would endeavour. . . .

Firstly, to show the preparations the world is making for *attack*, from the purely physical point of view.

Secondly, to show the preparations the world is making for *defence*, from the same point of view.

Thirdly, . . . but wait a minute.

The object of these first *two* parts of the book would be to arrive at some *definite* conclusion as to the result of the next war. There is a school of thought which maintains that another world war might destroy all life, human and animal, over a large surface of the globe. There is another school which categorically denies this suggestion, sneers at it as 'an H. G. Wells fantasy' and gains comfort by the old military dogma that 'methods of defence always march at an equal pace with methods of attack'. There is yet another school, which numbers among its adherents such eminent men as Mr. G. D. H. Cole, which maintains that the real danger to Europe is not another gigantic war, but a series of small wars, which will exhaust the body politic, like running sores, and prepare the way for a disintegration which will be no less complete because it is gradual.

It seems to me that the perfect book must try to come to some sort of conclusion on these two questions.

Thirdly, the ideal book on this subject, having arrived as nearly as possible at some authoritative opinion on the probable character and result of 'the next war', would examine the various forces and organizations which are working for peace, and . . .

Fourthly, the author would make up his mind as to what should be his own attitude in the circumstances.

However, to write such a book in the present state of Europe is well-nigh impossible. Constantly, the framework is torn from under one's feet by the swirling tide of contemporary events. You yourself, who have so often played the role of prophet, will sympathize with my humble difficulties. Last year, for example, I was at some pains to discover the probable characteristics of the Hitler regime, should Hitler ever come to power. I spent a great deal of time and money in Germany, and at last I gathered a number of startling facts which I introduced into a chapter of this book. That chapter is now in the waste-paper-basket, because all the facts, and all the prophecies, are already commonplace. And by the time these words are published, it is quite possible that Hitler may be exiled from his own country, a discredited pantaloon, twiddling his swastika in a glass of cheap champagne somewhere on the Côte d'Azur. Or, again, he may have repudiated the homicidal lunatics who surround him, and have pulled himself, and Germany, together. I have torn up so many pages of manuscript, and the wild winds of 1933 have blown so many others out of the window, that I shall leave these words to stand. Even if they are of no other value, they are evidence of the feverish condition of the age in which I write.

Part one, therefore, was obviously impossible. So I have concentrated on a few permanent evils, such as the armament industry. The public don't know much about this. My close-up of an armament firm at work will, I feel, be valuable, whatever the next few months will bring.

Part two offered fewer difficulties. I have always been suspicious of military dogmas, and the dogma about the powers of defence developing equally with the powers of attack seemed to me particularly vulnerable in these days, in view of the tremendous acceleration of deadly mechanical devices, and the daily increasing mobility and effectiveness of the aerial arm. To put it crudely, I was prepared to hazard a pretty shrewd guess that for every man who was engaged in manufacturing gas masks there would be at least a hundred men engaged in manufacturing poisonous gases, directly or indirectly. I was also prepared to guess that though large portions of the 'civilian' population, in every country, were being trained in offensive tactics, practically no preparations were being made to train them in defence, . . . to show them, for example, what measures to take if a bomb drops in their street, and their house begins to be permeated with Lewisite.

I know, of course, that the margin between 'defence' and 'offence' is vague and indeterminate, and that the military mind pretends that every sort of weapon, in every country, is purely 'defensive,' even if it is a gun with a range of 100 miles, trained across the channel.

But to the layman there is at least a workable distinction between offence and defence. A gun is offensive, a steel helmet is not. What are we doing about our steel helmets? That is really the gist of the matter. My researches proved to me that we were doing practically nothing at all. They showed me a mad world, in which the madmen were all thinking of swords, and none of them were thinking of armour.

IV

Part three — the examination of those organizations which are working for peace — should really have been written by you, because you are the only living man who combines the bird's eye view with the microscopic. And yet, in some ways, it is better that I should have done it, because in these matters, the very stumbling of the writer may make it easier for the reader to keep pace with him.

There is only one thing to be said in favour of this part of the book — that I believe it makes the idea of the League of Nations less boring than it usually is. For years I have yawned whenever I read the word 'Geneva'. It seemed to me the apotheosis of everything that was dull. This is, of course, as the majority of the British lords of the press would wish it to be. Geneva is anathema to them, for reasons which I am still at a loss to understand.

From here onwards the book is taken out of my hands. Other voices are heard, lifted in argument. I record and listen. Finally, I hope, I make up my mind. We had better leave it at that, or you will get bored with this letter. And the reader will have his hopes unwarrantably aroused, because, as I have observed before, this is not a book, only a few desperate inquiries, by one who, in the past, has been pleased to use his pen only as an instrument to trace pretty patterns, . . . not as a battering ram to break down the ugly walls of prejudice.

V

However, before you do me the honour of reading these pages, of which, I should explain, you have no sort of knowledge and for which you must be held in no way responsible, except by the inspiration of your published works — before you do me the honour of reading these pages, I would suggest that it is necessary for both of us to clarify our definitions of certain words. You have always been scrupulous in this matter. If a word seemed to you blurred, defaced, or chipped, if it seemed to you to have ceased to ring true, you polished it, stamped on it, yes, you even spat on it, as though it were a coin, before flinging it on the counter of public opinion. For words, after all, are the coins of thought. And passion twists them till they lose their value, and are indistinguishable from the counterfeit.

This is a book about WAR. It is a passionate endeavour to clear up a few of the problems which are agitating the mind of a very average man — agitating him so much that he has to set aside the writing of plays and novels, in order to get this thing settled. And therefore it seems vital that the word WAR should be clearly defined, unless we are going to argue at cross-purposes. I would therefore bring the following suggestion to your notice:

Until August, 1914, the word 'war' meant to the nations of the world what it had always meant, since the days of Napoleon . . . indeed, since the days of Hannibal. When, on August 22nd, 1914, a half-squadron of the fourth dragoon guards established contact with the enemy at Soignies – (where, from the church tower, the field of Waterloo was just visible) – their tactics would have been fully familiar to the shade of Wellington, though it is to be hoped that Wellington would have been slightly pained by the fact that the 'enemy' of 1914 was the 'ally' of 1815. The 'enemy' was largely composed of Bavarian ploughboys in German uniforms. They carried long metal lances, which they could not manage very well. Some of the English dragoons, in pursuing them, had refrained at first from running some of them through, because their backs were turned.

On that Saturday morning, when the sun sparkled so brightly on the canal that stretches from Mons to Condé, the word 'war', in the dictionaries of the world, still rang true. It was still morally, tactically and mechanically significant. Morally, because the old chivalry was still alive. It died inevitably, a little later, and for ever. Chivalry was a flower too fine to blossom for long on the poisoned fields of Flanders. That there was magnificent and incredible individual sacrifice and heroism, on both sides, no man in his senses will deny. But chivalry, as a unifying, purifying spirit fled affrighted from all the armies at last, whether of the Allies or of the central powers.

That Saturday was one of the last Saturdays, on this planet, when the word 'war' was still invested with a certain morality. It was also one of the last Saturdays when it still bore the remotest resemblance to the wars of the past. For already, the shade of Wellington, watching from the adjoining fields of Waterloo, would have been puzzled by a strange noise that came neither from the right nor the left, but from overhead. Looking up, he would have seen a German and an English plane, firing viciously at one another. And he would have gazed in astonishment at the first real drama of the air that the world had seen.

Now, as soon as the first shot in the air was fired the word 'war' became obsolete. It should have been struck out of the dictionaries of the world, and a new word should have been put in its place, a word which was not narrowed to the historical interpretation of armies in conflict, but which could be applied to the latest possibilities of blowing up babies in Baghdad by pressing a button in Birmingham. Needless to say, the obsolescence of the word was not immediately apparent — it was not indeed till the final days of Armageddon that we realized how completely new was this vile and hideous thing which had us in its grip. And even then, only a few minds realized it. The majority of the English people, even in the middle of an air-raid, still carried a subconscious mental image of 'war' as a fight of one group of men against another group of men, whereas the image they *should* have carried was the universal struggle of all mankind against a common enemy, an enemy whose arms were steel and whose breath was a sickly, yellow death.

VI

But how could any man carry the right image of war in his head when every schoolmaster under whom he had ever sat had striven so sedulously to implant the wrong one? 'William the Conqueror, 1066' . . . through endless summer afternoons the little boys of England have chanted the familiar jingle, while the flies crawled up the windows and the class-room was sleepy with the tang of new-mown hay. They chanted it before the war, they chant it still, and across their young brains there flashes the silver of ancient swords, over the shallow waters of their understanding there flutters the reflected gold of flags flying in forgotten winds, and down the long corridors of youth there echoes a sweet trumpet call to battle.

Of course, they have been to war-films, and have seen young men in really dreadful pain . . . such pain that the grease-paint ran down the actor's cheeks as he crawled over the papier mâché trench. Oh, yes — the little boys have seen war-films, and they have loved them . . . loved the flags that always flared so bravely, at the end, across the skies of Hollywood, while the canned music filled the auditorium with the strains of the Star Spangled Banner, the Marseillaise, or more rarely, God Save the King, inaccurately harmonized. They have seen these films, and they have gone out clutching their fathers' hands, into the noisy streets, past placards announcing 'The Greatest Anti-War Film of History'. And as they pass those placards you see that their young faces are flushed with the beauty of it all, you see, in their bright eyes, the old flash of silver lances. 'War' is still, to the historian, to the politician, and to the film-director, a grand and inspiring affair.

We want another word. What is it to be? It must be a word devoid of decency, and a word devoid of sense. A word with no historical associations, carrying no sonorous echoes of tragic beauty. A word trailing no clouds of glory. There is no such word. And the only phrase which truly expresses the situation is 'mass murder of civilians'. It is a clumsy phrase, but even so, it is better than the word 'war'. There is hardly a single living authority who attempts to deny that the next war will be largely decided in the air, and that the first and main object of any air force will be to paralyse the enemy's nerve centres — i.e. to destroy the chief enemy towns. This will involve, needless to say, the mass murder of civilians.

If you take this phrase and substitute it for the word 'war', you arrive at some grotesque conclusions. You are forced to face the fact that 'the mass murder of civilians' is an extremely odd way of settling international problems, to say the least of it. It is easy enough to make beautiful speeches about 'war' — Mr. Asquith, for example, made very pretty play with his unsheathed sword on more than one occasion in August, 1914. But if, instead of the phrase, 'we shall not sheathe the sword' he had used the phrase, 'we shall not desist from gassing babies', the emotions of his audience might not have been so exalted. That is what any honest statesman, in any country, will have to say about a future 'war'. And therefore I think that one of the greatest services any millionaire could render to mankind would be the offer of a substantial prize to any man who invented a slogan that would finally drive this cheating word 'war' out of the currency of decent contemporary language.

VII

And now, 'I must close', as one used to say in letters from school. And I have a very schoolboy feeling about the little book which follows, because I fear you may be tempted to mark it 'gamma minus'.

Yet, it had to be written. And there are many thousands of young men in this country who, if they had the time, would work out some similar confession of faith. For they feel, as I do, that life is not worth living, under this shadow of war. The Spring is poisoned, the Summer is made a mockery, the Winter is a dark time of threatening winds and haunting dreads. All that is gay and lovely in life is tainted. How can a man think, let alone dream, when the hills and valleys are filled with the echo of soldiers' marching? How can he build a house, when the very soil is trembling beneath his feet? How can he have the heart to save a fortune, or plant a fair garden? How, even, can he make love, in this shadow, which broods over all human life like a monstrous phantom?

Enough of these questions. We had better plunge straight into the heart of the problem. And the heart of the problem, as I see it, is the armament industry.

There lies on my desk a little report issued by the

League of Nations.[1] Quite a modest document. It was published twelve years ago, and after a few copies had fluttered round the offices of Europe, it was politely filed and forgotten.

League of Nations reports are usually boring in the extreme. But this one is of so sensational a nature that if it had received proper publicity it would have shaken Europe. For here are the hideous accusations which it makes:

1. That armament firms have fomented war-scares.
2. Have attempted to bribe government officials.
3. Have spread false reports concerning military and naval programmes of foreign countries in order to stimulate armament expenditure.
4. Have sought to influence public opinion through control of the press.

If you ponder these accusations, and read between the lines, you will see, gradually dawning, a picture for which the adjective 'hideous' is mild. But it will be only a misty picture. I want to fill it in — to give it light and colour and movement. And so I am now going to take you on a journey. We will get in a train, and travel to a destination which must remain anonymous, and these are the first words which we shall hear . . . .

[1] The First Sub-Committee of the Temporary Mixed Commission of the League of Nations. Report A. 8, 1921,

CHAPTER II

THE BLOODY INTERNATIONAL (DEATH, LTD.)

'Of course, this is a novelty, so we get a better price for it.'

I stood in the armament factory, staring at the 'novelty,' which was a new sort of floating mine. It was a particularly horrible variety. Any submarine which brushed against it would instantly be annihilated. The bodies of the crew would hurtle, in fragments, through the reddening water.

Yet this 'novelty' only cost about £300.

Pretty good business that, to kill fifty sailors for £300. It works out at only £6 per sailor. Of course, there are transport charges to consider, because these British mines were going to places as far distant as the Balkans and South America. Still, even if the net cost worked out at as much as £7 per sailor, it would still be good business. Especially if the sailors who are blown up are British, as they well may be. British sailors, one imagines, cannot be worth much less than £7 apiece.

The factory where I saw this mine forms the starting-point of our pilgrimage. It is one of many that are scattered all over England. There is nothing secret about the activities of these institutions – in fact, members of the public can inspect an armament works almost as easily as they can inspect a chocolate factory. They will not be shown any secrets, of course, any more than the head of a chocolate firm will hand out to tourists his new formula for coffee creams. However there is no need to be shown secrets. The open facts are quite frightening enough.

It is very essential, if you are going to read this book with any profit, that you should get a clear idea of the armament industry at work. I myself had only a very hazy notion, when I began. I knew that guns and submarines, and bombing aeroplanes, and all that sort of thing, were being made by private firms, but I vaguely imagined that they must be under some sort of government control. I certainly did not realize that the entire business was unfettered and competitive. I did not realize that in our midst were these vast corporations, trading in death, profiting by death, owing their very existence to death. The fact that these firms also trade in pleasure steamers, etc., does not alter the fact that, with many of them, the main trade is in *death*.

In case this idea is too shocking for you to grasp, at first — it took me some time to grasp it — let me suggest a parallel which may possibly make it more vivid to you. Supposing that some enterprising journalist, wandering in a desolate part of northern England, came across an old castle inhabited by a lunatic scientist. Supposing that by some means or other he obtained admission to the castle, wormed his way into the madman's secrets, and then made the horrifying discovery that he was preparing to wipe out the entire population of London by an invention which would infect the whole city with a new and agonizing disease. Supposing that he overpowered the scientist, in the true Edgar Wallace manner, rushed out of the castle, across the windswept moor, to the little village in the valley, woke up the landlord of the inn, and got through to London on the telephone. Can't you see the headlines of this scoop in the following morning's *Daily Blank?*

Daily Blank Saves London's Millions
Incredible Plot of Mad Scientist
Germs That Would Have Killed Millions

Yes, laugh, if you think it funny. The days when any of us will be able to laugh are so tragically few that we may as well make the most of them. For the journalistic story I have suggested is a dull trifle, compared with the truth.

II

Armsville[1] is a flourishing town. Armsville is in clover. There are unemployed of course . . . in fact, one of the foremen, when he was showing me over a gun factory, apologized because '*things are so quiet now!*' It struck me as one of the queerest apologies I had ever heard. As though the matron of a cancer hospital should heave a sigh and say . . . 'we're *so* sorry . . . some of the beds

[1] Although this is a photographically accurate report of my visit to a certain armament factory, I shall use the pseudonym of Armsville, partly for personal reasons, but principally because a few incidents in the report are incorporated from visits to other and similar factories. The word Armsville is however the only touch of fiction in the report.

are empty . . . there's been rather a falling off lately . . . still we live in hopes!'

However, although Armsville is flourishing, it is grim. The skies look as though they have been scattered with ashes. The air is tainted. The whole place was particularly depressing on the morning I visited it. The wind moaned round the sheds and the outbuildings, like a dying man, and the rain lashed down with the fury of a barrage.

I was shown over by the foreman of the works. And since he was a charming man, doing his job efficiently and well, I felt a little guilty, like a spy. And so, in order to set my conscience at rest, and to make my position quite plain at the outset, I said to him:

'I don't want to see anything that I oughtn't to see . . . nothing private . . . you understand.'

'That's all right,' he said. 'You won't!'

Which in a way, reassured me.

And yet, on the walls of the office, there was hanging a document which I should have thought would have been very private indeed. As it apparently wasn't . . . for anybody who walked in there could have seen it, staring him in the face . . . it would seem to be no breach of confidence to reproduce it. It was the firm's 'Estimates' . . . i.e. a chart of the work which they had recently been undertaking. These estimates were numbered, and each item bore the date when the objects being manufactured were due. The dates and the numbers need not concern us, but it may be interesting to note one fact about its activities. This is how this great English firm . . . (in only one of its branches, remember)

. . . has recently been contributing to civilization . . . by supplying instruments of death to no less than fourteen governments simultaneously. Two of these governments were, at that very moment, actually engaged in hostilities. Yet, Armsville was supplying them both!

III

Now, before we go any further over this factory, are you beginning to see that there was a certain reason for giving this chapter such a very blunt title? I called it 'The Bloody International'. Well, you will hardly deny that it is international. And it is a little difficult to see how you can avoid calling it bloody — unless you think that such things as mines are laid in the water for purely decorative purposes. So what else is it but a bloody international — this trade?

If you can think of a better title I shall be glad to hear of it.

And now let us continue our tour of the factory.

The first things I saw of any interest were housed in an immense barn-like building, which was in a perpetual state of uproar owing to the furious activity of the riveters next door. We had to shout to make ourselves heard. And so, when I saw these odd-looking guns, standing in a corner, I yelled:

'What are these?'

The guns were very complicated and ingenious-looking. They were beautifully camouflaged in greys and yellows and blues.

'Anti-aircraft guns for Turkey.'

'Really?'

I approached them more closely. So although this firm was working for Greece, it was also working for Greece's hereditary enemy, Turkey! The good old tradition, you see! For was it not Sir Basil Zaharoff who sold the world's first submarine to Greece? And then took the first boat to Turkey and persuaded the Turks that since Greece had one submarine, Turkey must have two? And thereby started the great submarine race which nearly destroyed the British Empire? Zaharoff was a 'patriot' honoured by the Empire which had nearly been brought to its knees by the results of his business. I am a pacifist, honoured by nobody. But which of us, in the long run, will be judged to have fought best for his country?

'Anti-aircraft guns for Turkey.'

There was a momentary lull in the riveting operation and I examined the guns more closely. Their muzzles were pointed to the skies. They looked queerly devotional, pointing upwards like that . . . as though they had been frozen in a moment of prayer. Tranquil, they looked, as though they could never do any harm to anybody.

'Yes. The Turks are terrified of everybody.'

'So you do a good business with them?'

'Pretty good.'

I took another look at the guns. It was difficult to realize that they had been created in order to search the skies, perhaps for Englishmen, and bring them down to earth in blazing, screaming death. They looked so nice and peaceful. The sort of thing a woman might put in her hall, if she had a big modern house.

There was an inscription, in Turkish, on the platforms of the machine. Beautifully engraved on a shiny brass plate. I wondered who had written it. Some retiring professor of languages, I expect. Perhaps he came from Cambridge.

'To fire the gun . . . pull back lever A . . . press button C . . .' And then, when he had written it, in Turkish, he looked out on to the green spaces of King's, congratulated himself on having made a couple of guineas, and went in to have a sole and a glass of sherry in the dimly lit hall. And somewhere, somehow, some boy shivered, because he felt a sudden dizziness, a quick, fleeting agony, as though he were falling . . . falling . . .

IV

We walked on. Ahead of us loomed a gigantic gun — the biggest I had yet seen in this frightening place. It was mounted on a high platform, proudly. It was superbly modelled, and it gleamed with new paint. It looked every inch an aristocrat . . . and there were fifty feet of it! Yet it was not an aristocrat. Indeed it spelt death to aristocrats, for it was destined for the Republic of Spain. Already twelve of its sisters had been dispatched to that turbulent country. Thirteen guns, with a range of thirty miles, firing fifteen-inch shells, each shell costing £100. Not for nothing did Spain cast off the yoke of monarchy, and join the revolutionary 'brotherhood' of mankind.

But what does it matter, to these firms, whether they deal death to monarchies or republics, to blacks or to whites, as long as they deal death? One of the overseers said to me, as I stared at this gun . . . '*We don't care who's having a whack at whom, providing we get the order!*'

And yet the young man who made this incredible remark was a decent, kindly fellow, with an open face and an engaging smile. The sort of chap you would trust. The sort that would not willingly be cruel to any living thing. That is one of the most tragic aspects of the armament trade — it takes fine men, and perverts them to its own horrible uses. For if you translate that young man's remark into another sphere you will see how unconsciously ghastly it is. It is as though an undertaker, during an epidemic of some disease, were to rub his hands together and chortle, 'We don't care who dies, old or young, provided we get the order!' That is really not an exaggerated parallel.

On and on we went, through hall after hall, out into the windswept yards, back again, upstairs, downstairs. I lost track of the number of things I saw. There were stacks of machine-guns for Bolivia, ready for dispatch. There was a room where machines of amazing delicacy measured instruments of death to within a thousandth of an inch. The mine episode I mentioned at the beginning of the chapter. It was that which really impressed me most of all, because it was so very obvious that these mines which were being sold to foreign governments, would serve their main purpose against the British navy.

The mines were evidently the factory's favourite. They were patted affectionately. They looked quite pretty — painted pale grey, hanging up there, so still and sleek. I'm sorry. I can't go on describing these hideous things. It gets me down. You have seen enough for the moment. Let us draw a line, and sum up the significance of this first step that we have taken together.

V

You have read a brief description of a private armament firm, one of a number of similar firms scattered over England.

This firm is unfettered. There is no sort of restraint on its activities. True, an export licence has to be obtained from the Foreign Office before armaments can be exported, but this licence can usually be obtained for the asking. The diversity of the governments to whom, as we have seen, arms are being supplied is proof enough of this fact, if proof is needed.

Well, what does it mean? This is a business world, and people don't work for nothing. What then is the crude, dirty truth behind the walls of these places? The truth is — more death, more dividends.

More death, more dividends! More blood — more bonuses! Each shell that screams across the sky . . . no matter over what forsaken country that sad sky may lower . . . is bringing money into the pockets of the Armsville shareholders. Perhaps only a penny or two, but every little helps. Thus may the men in Bolivia, in Rumania, in Italy, or wherever the Armsville writ may run, console themselves. Their entrails are blown out? Their leg is hanging by the knee? A 'portion of the brain is protruding' — (as the medical reports so often delicately described it?) No matter. Some nice old soldier's widow in Bournemouth can buy a few extra flowers for her husband's grave next Christmas, because Armsville's are paying their dividend as usual.

This is bitter writing, but the facts are as bitter as the taste of stale blood. Facts — you say? These things *can't* be facts. Over and over again I have said the same to myself, laying down my pen, staring at the wall in front of me, asking myself when I am going to wake from this hideous nightmare. But it is no nightmare. I am not dreaming. The clock still ticks on the wall. Outside, the wind whirls and scurries in the giant elms, and the leaves that drift over the moonlit paths are real leaves that smell sharp and fragrant when you go out and crush them in your hands, to cool the fever in your blood.

Facts. That the government of this country, of every country, allows vast corporations to trade in death. That the government of this country, of every country, while raising its black-gloved hands in horror at the White Slave Traffic, at the Drug Traffic, at all other illegal traffics, yet gives its approval, its honour and blessing, to the traffic in death. If you can give me a more accurate description of a private armament firm, I shall be greatly obliged. However, I regret to say that you can't. A man who sells, at a profit, instruments for the destruction of other men, is a trafficker in death. The more instruments he sells the more profit he will make. Therefore, the more men who are killed, disembowelled, blinded, or otherwise rendered incapable of enjoying the dubious privileges of existence on this odd planet, the better he will be pleased. If you deny this, you deny that men like making money, which is really too much to ask me to believe. And so, like a problem in Euclid, the matter is solved.

It needs a strong man to face such a solution without hanging his head in shame for the human race.

CHAPTER III

MYSTERY AT LE CREUSOT

THE car sped through the heart of the wine country. As every kilometre flashed by, the rickety signboards revealed magic names . . . Nuits-Saint-Georges, Pommard, Chambertin. As far as the eye could see, there were brown, rolling fields, thickly planted with vines. And since the first pale sun of spring was shining, and the sweet sap stirring, there was a sense of faint intoxication in the keen air, a suggestion of *bouquet* in the wind that blew through the open window.

I needed this refreshment, because I was on a mission which was not at all agreeable. I was about to visit the great factory of the Schneider armament company at le Creusot, and I was visiting it in the capacity of a spy.

You might have thought that after the visit to 'Armsville,' I had seen enough of armament factories. In some ways that is true, but it seemed to me very necessary to give the reader an impression of the way in which these firms spread their tentacles over Europe, and France was the obvious starting-point. France is quite literally governed by the Comité des Forges . . . that sinister association of ironmasters whose influence is the more poisonous for being so secret. The French press is largely in the grip of the armament manufacturers, and criticism is silenced, so that, even the most appalling accusations against the Comité receive little publicity. As an example of this conspiracy I may quote the accusation of that great socialist deputy Barthé, as reported in a fine article by the *Daily Herald's* Paris correspondent on March 31st, 1933:

Barthé explained to a hushed House how the Comité des Forges wilfully limited the development of the production of iron and steel before 1914, so that when the war came it might exploit the scarcity with profit. In this way Germany was favoured and France imperilled.

'I affirm,' he added, 'that certain members of the Comité des Forges furnished raw material to Germany during the war and that in order to conceal the affair the Comité hindered the investigations of Justice.

'I affirm that either through the international solidarity of the great metallurgical industry or in order to safeguard private interests an order was given to our military chiefs not to bombard the Briey Valley factories which were operated by the enemy during the war.'

Immune from attack, the Briey region furnished material for guns which slaughtered French and British troops. Germany would have capitulated in 1915, its iron-masters have since admitted, if Briey had been bombarded.

These accusations have never been refuted. People don't even seem to care. Why? I can only conclude that it is because they do not realize what men like Barthé are talking about. These things are merely vague generalizations to them. They do not visualize these factories, nor smell them, nor hear the sound of their whirling wheels.

They cannot form a picture of endless crates of arms and shells, labelled with destinations that cover the face of the globe.

I found it difficult to realize these things myself. And that is why I went to le Creusot.

In order to obtain permission to visit this factory I had been forced to go first to Geneva, and to spend a fairly long time there, pulling strings. However, the strings had eventually responded, and one day, I was informed that the French War Office had telegraphed to Geneva, saying that I had only to present myself at the factory to be shown anything I cared to see. Whereupon I took the first train to Dijon, slept at the famous Hotel de la Cloche, and set out, on the following morning, to le Creusot, which lies about fifty miles to the south-west.

As we sped through the wine country, I asked myself, once again, a question which had been perturbing me ever since I left Geneva. Why had Schneider-Creusot apparently thrown open its doors in this disarming fashion? Why had the War Office in Paris apparently given me its blessing? Schneider-Creusot were presumably averse to meddling strangers. Their works, which were scattered all over France, were supposed to be difficult to enter. Whether you went to Creusot itself or Havre or Londe-les-Maures or Bordeaux, or any of the other factories, you might well be met with a polite refusal. Armament makers shun publicity, for reasons too obvious to enumerate. Why, then, was I to be allowed to wander about as I pleased? I had a sudden presentiment that things were not going to be as easy as they had seemed at Geneva. Therefore I sat up in the car, and began to take notes of any little detail which might be of assistance.

Suddenly, the vine country ceased. We climbed a wooded hill. Soon I saw a ball of smoke on the horizon. 'Le Creusot,' said the driver, jerking his thumb in the direction of the smoke. I nodded. We sped on, until the long straggly town loomed before us.

And here, right on the outskirts, was one detail which was extremely significant. Or rather, hundreds upon hundreds of details, in the shape of new workmen's dwellings, which had sprung up in the valley like mushrooms. They looked as if they had been erected only a few months ago. And this, in a time of unparalleled industrial depression, when every ordinary factory, all over the world, had been laying off workmen, shutting up plants, and, of sheer necessity, allowing employees to fend for themselves. Why this very exceptional state of affairs at le Creusot? Why was le Creusot so flourishing, in an otherwise stagnant world? The reader who remembers the similar prosperity of 'Armsville' in the last chapter, who recalls that it was a comparative oasis of activity on a desert coast, will not find it difficult to supply the answer.

II

We pulled up at a charming house, built of soft grey stone, and standing in a quiet courtyard.

'You are sure that this is the headquarters of the factory?' I asked the driver as I got out.

But yes. He was quite certain. He had often taken

other gentlemen to le Creusot. 'Foreign gentlemen,' he added.

I looked again at this house, which was more like a country vicarage than the chief office of an armament factory. Compared with the vast factories which stretched behind it, it seemed asleep, untroubled by the roar of distant furnaces, untarnished by the sullen cloud of smoke that hung above it.

I walked through the courtyard, and opened the door. I found myself in a lofty hall, thickly carpeted. And here, straight in front of me, were proofs that this was neither a vicarage nor a quiet country house, but a grimly utilitarian building. The proofs were in the shape of a row of shells, brightly painted in blues and reds and yellows. They had evidently been placed there for purposes of decoration. They were, indeed, so very decorative that no pangs of conscience could possibly assail the heart of any foreign minister who happened to visit le Creusot with the object of giving an order. How could the citizens of his country possibly object to having their money spent on such charming looking things? It would be almost a pleasure to be killed by them.

An attendant with one eye missing rose from the table and advanced towards me. I began to explain the object of my visit. He did not listen to me, nor did he look at me. He only walked slowly towards a door, opened it, and motioned me inside. I went in. The door shut, and I waited.

I waited and waited. How long, I do not know, but it seemed nearly half an hour. Suddenly, the door opened again, and another attendant appeared. I told him why I had come. He listened, gravely and respectfully, and then he departed. Another long wait. The walls were hung with photographs of shells, anti-aircraft guns, and other less objectionable objects, such as turbines and dynamos. On the wall opposite me hung a calendar, with little historical titbits under each date. I walked over to it, and looked at the tibtit for the day.

'Friday 18th.

'1814. Victory of Napoleon at Montereau.'

That was very appropriate, I felt. Victory of Napoleon at Montereau. And a lot of good it had done him, or anybody else. What was the titbit for to-morrow?

'Saturday 19th.

'1668. The Prince of Condé achieves the conquest of la Franche-Comte.'

Thus does mankind look forward! There was something extremely irritating in this calendar of tarnished glories, hanging underneath photographs showing factories stacked with shells, and guns of incredible power. I tore off those two dates, so that the calendar now informed all and sundry that it was the Sabbath, and I had a petulant and childish hope that some armament maker might look at it, think he had mistaken the date, and go home, ceasing his horrid activities for at least one extra day.

Still the clock ticked on. It was deadly quiet in this room. I wondered if all the clerks had died of some sort of poison gas.

Then the door opened again, admitting a man of distinguished appearance, grey-haired, nicely dressed, wearing the ribbon of the Legion of Honour.

Yes? And what could he do for me?

I explained once again.

He regarded me with evident fatigue. He did not understand. No letter had arrived. I was not, by any chance, Mr. Simmons?

By no chance was I Mr. Simmons, I assured him.

Mr. Simmons, observed the beribboned gentleman, was a technician.

And a very good one, too, I expect, but . . .

Mr. Simmons, he added, was to have visited the factory three weeks ago, and . . .

But, I insisted, I wished to visit it this afternoon, and I had received a definite assurance, from a person of complete integrity, that the War Office in Paris had wired instructions that I was to be admitted. The telephones had been busy from Geneva to Paris, I told him. I began to speak a little wildly. I told him that I had come a good many hundred miles, at considerable expense, to visit his factory. I mentioned the name of a distinguished Minister, who, I had been assured at Geneva, had interested himself on my behalf.

All to no effect. The only result was that my friend rose slowly from his chair, asked me if I would be obliging enough to wait, and left the room.

And now my suspicions deepened. Schneiders, I imagined, must have been warned that a rampant pacifist was about to storm their gates. Quite naturally, they preferred me to keep outside. Armament makers, as any secret service agent will tell you have their spies in every country. It seemed only too likely that spies had not been inactive, and that my name had been put on a dossier of undesirables.

As I sat in that office, these suspicions were still only vague and uncrystallized. Had I known then what the next few months were to bring me, I should have been more certain. For constantly, in my travels, doors which had been thrown open to me, in advance, were suddenly and mysteriously closed.

There was an occasion in Belgium for example, where after endless trouble, I obtained the entrée into a certain prison in order to interview certain young men who are undergoing sentences of the utmost brutality for their refusal to comply with the military service acts. Everything I was told, had been arranged, down to the last detail. I went to Belgium. Everything *had* been arranged. But at the last moment, the door was shut, by some mysterious hand, and the prison was never opened to me. I could cite a dozen similar instances, but it would take too long, and it is not really relevant to the story.

What *is* relevant is that at last my distinguished friend appeared again, and handed me to a guide who took me off to see a lot of motor car parts being made.

Yes! That was the one and only result of my visit to le Creusot! A walk through a vast foundry in which a number of sweating workmen were striking sparks from pieces of molten metal!

'Mais les matériels d'artillerie?' I asked the guide.

'Non monsieur.'

'Les obusiers et les mortiers?'

'Non monsieur.'

'Les obus à balles, les bombes d'avion?'

'Non monsieur.'

And after each 'non monsieur' he waved his hand with charming grace in the direction of a molten mudguard.

III

I drove back to Dijon cursing. Somebody had made me look a pretty fool. However I had not finished with them yet. Even if they would not allow me into their confidence, there were plenty of other sources of information available. For some days I busied myself with an examination of these sources. Here are a few facts about this firm which may interest the reader.

The factory at Creusot, from the point of view of war material, is, strangely enough, the least important. The chief war factory is at Havre. It was acquired by Schneiders in 1897 and has since been enormously developed. However there is also considerable activity at the workshops of Châlons-sur-Saone, and also at Londe-les-Maures. At Creux-Saint-Georges, near Toulon, they make submarines, at Bordeaux artillery parts. Nor is this all.

For the Schneider web is not woven only over France. The Schneider combine also control the great Skoda works in Czecho-Slovakia. Now this means more than appears on the surface, for not only are the Skoda enterprises scattered all over Czecho-Slovakia, but the Skoda company also has factories in Poland (e.g. many of its aeroplane engines are made in Warsaw), and in Rumania. Indeed its activities might almost be said to extend to America, for Wright aeroplanes, as supplied to the

American government, are manufactured by the Polskie Zaklady Skoda. Quite a large family, is it not?

But it is a family affair in a more literal sense. You will find directors from Schneiders sitting complacently on the boards of banks all over the world. On Japanese banks, Argentine banks, Turkish banks. Heaven knows in what banks you *won't* find a director from Schneiders. Eugène Schneider himself, the chairman, is a director of the Banque de l'Union Parisienne, which finances the Banque Générale de Credit Hongrois.

Now listen! In case you are beginning to yawn over this, here is a little plot, exposed for you, which is as villainous as anything in melodrama. You will find it unobtrusively printed in that sober and highly-honoured journal the *Manchester Guardian*, of December 14th, 1931. The *Guardian* referred, as follows, to a speech by Paul Faure, ex-M.P. for the Creusot division.

'The Hungarian government obtained a loan from the armament firm of Schneider at Creusot. (This loan was unknown until it was discovered the other day by the Finance Committee of the Chamber.) When Schneider's asked to be repaid the Hungarian government could not produce the money. *Thereupon the French Government lent the Hungarian Government the amount necessary to repay the Schneider firm.* This money was transmitted to Hungary by the Union Parisienne, in which the Schneider firm holds a controlling interest.'

Now listen again! You really ought to read that paragraph again, if you find your attention wandering. Will you please? Thank you! Because, although all this sounds very far away and foreign and remote and peculiar, it isn't. Just translate it — as we very reasonably may — to America and England. How does the parallel read? It reads like this:

The Bethlehem Steel Corporation makes a loan to the British Government of $100,000,000. When the Bethlehem Steel Corporation asks for its money back, the British Government refuses to pay. Whereupon the American government lends the British government $100,000,000, to repay the Bethlehem Steel Company, and transmits this money to England, not by the Federal Reserve Bank but by a bank which Bethlehem Steel controls.

That is a literal parallel to the little devil's game they are playing in Europe. What would happen if they played it in America? One hardly dares to think.

IV

Now I implore the reader, if he is bored, to skip the rest of this chapter, which is simply and solely concerned to rub in the lesson that armament firms are one of the world's greatest menaces to peace. If you have learnt that lesson, please turn on to Chapter IV. If not, here is some important evidence which you may care to bring to the attention of your friends who hold shares in armament concerns. (The shareholders, by the way, are eminently respectable. More than one bishop supplements the income he obtains from serving the Prince of Peace by also investing in the business of the God of War.)

Let us preface this evidence by a quotation from no less an authority than M. Briand, who cried, shortly before his death:

'*The pens which write against disarmament are made of the same steel as that from which guns are made!*'

And then, let us once more remind you of the League of Nations accusations, as mentioned in my letter to H. G. Wells:[1]

1. That armament firms have fomented war-scares.
2. Have attempted to bribe government officials.
3. Have spread false reports concerning military and naval programmes of foreign countries in order to stimulate armament expenditure.
4. Have sought to influence public opinion through control of the press.

V

It would take a whole book to verify all these accusations. We will therefore refer only to one scandal which has come to light, in which all these four charges are justified. This is

THE SHEARER CASE

Since most English people have never heard of this case, while the American public is very hazy about the facts, we will give a nutshell edition of this pretty little drama.

[1] By far the richest source of information on the statistics of armament firms is *The Secret International* published by The Union of Democratic Control at 34 Victoria Street, S.W.1, price 6d. Without the aid of this booklet, both in providing facts and suggesting further avenues of information, this chapter could never have been written.

Mr. Shearer was an American gentleman who was described as a 'publicist' — a term that frequently covers a multitude of sins. In 1929 he sued the three largest shipbuilding corporations in America. . . .

The Bethlehem Shipbuilding Corporation.

The Newport News Shipbuilding and Drydock Company.

The American Brown Boveri Corporation.

For the trifling sum of $255,655.

This sum he claimed as the balance due to him for his services in preventing any effective disarmament resulting from the Naval Conference in Geneva in 1927.

He admitted that he had already received $51,230.

He claimed the remainder as a reward for his skill in influencing orders for battleships which would never have been built if the Disarmament Conference had proved successful.

In September, 1929, President Hoover instructed the Attorney-General to make an inquiry, and shortly afterwards Eugene Grace, who was then president of the Bethlehem Shipbuilding Corporation, wrote to the President and explained that Mr. Shearer had been employed as an 'observer', at a fee of $25,000.

An 'observer'.

Which raises the immediate question, what did Mr. Shearer 'observe' that was so very valuable to this armament firm? He did not go there to write sonnets about the lake. He did not go there to paint pen pictures of the passing shadows that flitted over the eyes of Lord Cecil. His 'observations' were not valuable for any literary reason. They were valuable — to the admitted extent of

$25,000 — for another reason. That reason has been conveniently summarized in Mr. Charles A. Beard's remarkable book *The Navy: Defense or Portent*, which did not cause nearly such a stir in America as it deserved:

(1) *For the employment of an 'observer' at the Geneva Arms Conference, who was notoriously engaged in violent anti-British propaganda, in doing his best to defeat arms limitation, in entertaining naval officers and American newspaper correspondents, in stimulating 'the marine industry, both for navy and the merchant marine' (to use his own words, Sen. Doc. p. 450), in sending out literature designed to discredit American advocates of peace, and in inserting his 'publicity' in reputable American newspapers under the guise of news* (ibid. p. 542).

(2) *For the purpose of influencing federal legislation by maintaining a lobby in Washington in support of cruiser and merchant-marine bills pending in Congress.*

(3) *For the preparation of political articles to be published in newspapers and magazines.*

(4) *For lectures before patriotic societies and other civic bodies.*

(5) *For the employment of 'experts' and other workers, whose exact activities are unknown.*

(6) *For addresses before the American Legion, Chambers of Commerce and similar organizations* (ibid. p. 635).

It may therefore be stated, without exaggeration, that the verb 'to observe' in the vocabulary of American armament manufacturers, has a peculiarly elastic conjugation.

VI

This tiresome examination is almost done. A few more facts and then we can get out into the streets again and breathe a little fresh air.

We have already done something to justify the accusations of the League of Nations Commission. However there is one point which must be shown more clearly, and that is the close connection between armament firms and governments — between these private enterprises and the executives of the states in which they work.

This requires a little explanation. Every government to-day has a paper scheme of its whole country mapped out as a vast arsenal, a scheme which is necessarily largely familiar to the armament firms, who are ready to go full steam ahead, when the hour comes. Even the pacific United States Government, for example, has gone to the length of preparing contracts with armament firms, to the number of some thousands. And the French Act of February, 1928, for the general organization of the country in war-time is so complete and thorough that it would bring tears of pious joy to the eyes of any armament director.

However the general principle, rather than the array of details, is the most convincing proof that governments and armament firms are, if not actually married, at least living together. Understand that principle and you understand the whole thing. It may be put in a very few words.

Since all armaments rapidly grow out of date, and . . .

Since no government can afford to be ill-equipped and . . .

Since, on the other hand, a constant scrapping of guns, aeroplanes, etc., would be beyond the budgetary capacity of any government . . .

It is therefore to the interest of any government that its own armament firms are kept as large, as alive, and as up to date as possible, and . . .

Armament firms can only do so by developing a large and regular peace-time export trade.

Now do you see what this implies? In case you do not, let us say, do you see what it does *not* imply? It certainly does not imply that any government in its senses . . . (I use the phrase 'in its senses' mindful of the fact that I am writing of a lunatic world . . .) will attempt to dissuade any armament firm from exporting arms to any country whatever. The more they export, the better the government concerned is pleased, because it means that their own firms are keeping their plants up to date, employing skilled workmen, and generally keeping up the high standard of their organizations, to which the government will have to turn when the hour comes. Thus we have the astonishing paradox of governments welcoming the fact that the whole world is being plastered with guns, etc., which have been exported from their own countries. They are apparently oblivious of the fact that these guns may one day explode in their own imbecile faces.

Now — that is untrue. They don't explode in the faces of the governments, but in the faces of the men who have to obey the governments. It is not unduly rhetorical to say that every time the English or the American or the French government signs a licence for the export of arms to a foreign country it is smashing, with its ugly fist, the young bodies of its own finest citizens. In case this sounds bitter, let me quote a speech which Mr. Hugh Dalton made in the House of Commons not long ago. He was speaking on the Naval Estimates, and was explaining how many Australian and British troops had been mowed down by British guns in the Dardanelles. In a moving passage, he cried:

'*British armament firms have been supplying the Turkish artillery with shells which were fired into the Australian, New Zealand and British troops as they were scrambling up Anzac Cove and Cape Helles. Did it matter to the directors of these armament firms, so long as they did business and expanded the defence expenditure of Turkey, that their weapons mashed up into bloody pulp all the morning glory that was the flower of Anzac, the youth of Australia and New Zealand, yes and the youth of our own country?*'

Apparently, it did not matter then, and it does not matter now. Neither to the armament firms, nor to the governments. For the licence is virtually a matter of form. A matter of form! It is a delicate way of describing the export of death.

Moreover, there appears to be no possibility of making public the number of licences granted, nor of obtaining particulars as to the countries to which the armaments are going. The League of Nations tried to enforce publicity in this matter, without success. There was a special commission, quite recently, which inquired as to the possibility of forcing governments to publish information as to the activities of their armament factories, by supplying full details, every quarter, to the Secretary-General of the League.

The British delegate gave the show away when, in response to this suggestion, he said:

'*We have no power to compel the manufacturers to give this information, and very few Governments would have the courage to make them do so.*'

The courage! The power! The governments haven't got it when they are face to face with Death Ltd. In fact, we have reached the horrible stage where the words of Undershaft, the armament maker, in Shaw's *Major Barbara*, are almost literally true. You remember the passage? It will form a fitting close for our chapter. . . .

'*The Government of your country! I am the Government of your country. Do you suppose that you and half a dozen amateurs like you, sitting in a row in that foolish gabble shop, govern Undershaft? No, my friend, you will do what pays us. You will make war when it suits us and keep peace when it doesn't . . . When I want anything to keep my dividends up, you will discover that my want is a national need. When other people want something to keep my dividends down, you will call out the police and military. And in return you shall have the support of my newspapers, and the delight of imagining that you are a great statesman.*'

CHAPTER IV

TO MAKE YOUR FLESH CREEP

It will be remembered that in my opening letter to Mr. H. G. Wells I suggested that the ideal book on the subject of peace and disarmament would be divided into four parts, of which the first part would be concerned with the world's preparations for *attack*, from a purely physical point of view, while the second part would be concerned with the world's preparations for *defence*, from the same point of view.

The reader will already have realized how far this collection of studies falls from perfection. It is now my melancholy task to inform him that even the design of the book must be changed. For this chapter is the last chapter devoted to showing the world's preparations for attack.

It is the last chapter, for very obvious reasons, which are proclaimed in almost every issue of almost every newspaper published in Europe to-day. Of what use is it for me to go on writing about the imminence of war when one can hardly hear oneself speak for the rattling of sabres? Of what use is it to delve deeper into national policies, to unearth secret service reports of hidden armies and illicit reserves when the Prime Minister of Great Britain has to leap into an aeroplane, scurry to Rome, and set all the telephone wires in Europe jangling with his passionate pleadings to various dictators, asking them to sheathe their swords for just a little longer? These things are so obvious, so universally admitted, that it would be superfluous to insist upon them.

On the very day I write, for example, there is a long and fully documented report in one newspaper, illustrating a chapter I had prepared but scrapped, showing the preparations which Germany is making for war. The Reichswehr, the regular German army, which is limited by the Treaty of Versailles to 100,000 men, is now organized in such a way that every regiment, in the event of mobilization, will automatically become a division. In fact, with the surplus police force and national military organizations, it is estimated that Germany would be able to put in the field, in the first few days of the war, a total of 550,000 men. In addition to this there is Hitler's army of 450,000, to say nothing of 1,600 shooting societies in the Stahlhelm, possessing 800,000 rifles.

It is only wearisome to dwell on these details. They are common knowledge. The Germans themselves do not attempt to deny them. For instance, when last I was in Paris, I saw a German propaganda film, made by Germans for Germans. Its French title was *Au delà du Rhin!* It was a quite unashamed exposé of the German Labour camps, which are scattered throughout the length and breadth of Germany. To give these camps, which are numbered by hundreds, the title of 'Labour', is merely farcical. They are entirely military organizations. The men are shown digging, yes, and digging with the energy of young giants. But at the end of every sequence they shoulder arms with their shovels, and march off to military drill. They are shown storming trenches — 'to keep fit' — charging with pikes — 'to keep fit '— singing 'Deutschland Uber Alles' — 'to keep fit'. One can only suppose that the Germans put in these naive sub-titles as a sort of grimly humorous commentary on the futility of trying to keep a great and proud people in perpetual bondage.

That is why the first part of this book, the part which describes the *offensive* preparations of the world, is so short. Because all the world knows that its neighbours are arming. You have only to go to any cinema, and see the weekly news-reel, to get enough evidence to convince the most optimistic pacifist. Every other picture shows an army on the march. The faces are the same, the figures are the same, the rhythm is the same, and they are all marching to the same destination — Death — for the same reason — Nothing. Only the flags are different. That is the reason why I have not considered it necessary to labour a point which is cruelly plain.

II

However, the average citizen, for whom this book is written, is easily lulled into a false security, even in the face of this universal marching and counter-marching, this sharpening of swords, and cocking of rifles. If he is a middle-aged man, living in a quiet suburb, it all seems rather remote. Of course, there may be air-raids, but they'll probably miss him. There may be a bombardment of Brighton or Scarborough. There may be food coupons again, and of course, the stock exchange will go to hell. But it won't last long. It *can't*, this time, he thinks. And of course, England will come out on top. She always does.

The actual prospect of personal pain, of tearing and gasping agony, seems unthinkable.

It is very far from being unthinkable. Indeed in any great war, it will be almost certainly inevitable. And the reason why it will be inevitable is contained in the one word — gas.

III

A great deal of nonsense has been written about gas in the next war. It is a word which, not unnaturally, makes people hysterical when they discuss it. And therefore it seems wiser that instead of drawing highly coloured pictures of babies growing black in the face, in quiet English houses, of whole counties being choked by a withering cloud that turns the hedgerows grey, I should first of all pay all due credit to that school of thought which contends that gas warfare is comparatively 'humane' and that its application on a wide scale is likely to be less appalling than is generally maintained.

The most eminent apostle of this school is Professor J. B. S. Haldane, who, I imagine, needs no introduction to any reader who is acquainted with the developments of modern science.[1] He and his disciples point out that

[1] For a complete exposition of Professor Haldane's point of view the reader should study *Callinicus, A Defence of Chemical Warfare*, published by Kegan Paul.

the casualties from the notorious mustard gas, for example, were only 150,000 in the British army, of which only some 4,000 died — a proportion of 1 in 40. Compared with this, shells kill one man for every three that they put out of action.

I think it is perfectly reasonable to contend, with the Haldane school, that large quantities of high explosives dropped on a great city are more likely to be immediately effective than poison gas. It is obvious that a really effective air-raid — (we have never yet been privileged to witness one in London) — would cause incalculable damage without the aid of gas at all. Apart from direct hits by shrapnel, or pieces of flying metal, large bodies of civilians would be suffocated or burnt to death. A modern edition of the Great Fire of London would, indeed, be a certainty. In the last war, when these things were in their infancy, the London fire brigades could cope with the situation. To-morrow, hardly the greatest optimist would suggest that they would be able to do so.

However, is this argument so very impressive? Is it so very comforting to be told that one will probably be burnt to death rather than gassed? Personally, I have no desire to end my life in either of these two fashions.

Besides, when you analyse the arguments of the pro-gas school, when you get them down to statistics, they are as misleading as the wildest prophecies of the most terrified pacifist. Professor Haldane, for example, in assuming the probable effect of a gas bombardment upon London, makes a rough calculation which is based on the preliminary German offensive of March 11th, 1918. It will be remembered that from March 11th to March

14th the Germans fired 150,000 mustard gas shells into the villages of the Cambrai Salient. He points out that this caused only 4,500 casualties, only fifty of which were fatal. He admits that had such a bombardment been directed against London, the casualties would '*Perhaps have been ten times greater, if the population had had gas masks*'. In other words, a mere 500 would have been killed, while 45,000 would be dispatched to the hospitals with blisters resembling cancer. Even this comparatively negligible prospect, however, 'would have required the visits, on repeated nights, of something like a thousand aeroplanes'. And, as Professor Haldane points out, such a number is not yet a practical possibility.

If you can gain any consolation from this argument, I envy you. Haldane's estimate of 500 dead (apart from the far greater number of dangerously wounded) is based on the assumption *that the whole population is wearing gas-masks*. As it is perfectly obvious that you could no more fit gas-masks to all the citizens of a great city, and expect them to continue functioning, than you could fit them to the birds of the air, this argument seems a little foolish.

You cannot eat or drink or speak when you are wearing a gas-mask. You can do nothing but sit tight, or lumber clumsily about. A minute proportion of the population might find refuge in shelters with filtered air — shelters which have yet to be built. The remainder would be defenceless.

It is hardly necessary to labour the point.

Yet, these arguments of Professor Haldane are the best that can be brought forward by a man with a brilliant mind who is definitely writing in *defence* of chemical warfare. I have not space to give full justice to his opinions. But if you acquaint yourself with his work, I believe that you will be forced to agree that his arguments are, to say the least of it, of a negative nature.

True, it is just as well that we should be reminded that the fatalities from mustard gas may be less than we expect. It is comforting to be told that the pain caused by such a gas as chlorine is small compared with the pain of a septic wound. It is reassuring to be told that an air-raid from a thousand aeroplanes is not yet practical politics. It is stimulating, also, to have it suggested that war would be made humane if no shells were used which contain anything but lachrymatory compound, and if all the armies were forbidden to wear goggles, so that they would merely be temporarily blinded. (Though how this pious hope is ever to be achieved is not told us!) But these are only, as I have suggested, negative arguments. Moreover they are contradicted by such a mass of expert opinion, that even so honourable a name as that of Professor Haldane ceases to impress us.

We will now examine that evidence.

IV

But first we must make up our minds on one very important point, namely, that gas *will* be used. Let there be no mistake about that! Let nobody hope that this time it will be a 'gentleman's war', nor that the flimsy paper declarations to which the statesmen have so constantly put their signatures will be able to withstand the white-hot flames of hatred which will instantly spring up from the scarred surfaces of Europe.

You can no more 'outlaw' gas than you can 'outlaw' the wind or the waves. Even if, by some miracle, you created a corporate conscience among the nations — even if you achieved an aim which is at present remote, i.e. the internationalization of all heavy industries and chemical factories, of every organization, that is to say, which is involved in the production and the distribution of this breath of the devil, the outbreak of war would put a quick end to these elegant agreements.

Some scatter-brained fool in a flying-machine would get hold of a mustard-gas bomb — (there are plenty lying handy) — and drop it on some crowded thoroughfare in a foreign city. Instantly, the outraged nation would be stung to general retaliation. Smoke would pour from all the chemical factories that are scattered over Europe. It would be a race against time . . . a race against a loathsome and unthinkable death.

Here we address ourselves once more to the common citizen. We may have made him feel slightly uncomfortable, but we have not yet made his flesh creep. For though he dislikes, intensely, the thought of a nasty, creepy, poisonous fog in his back garden, though he may be genuinely alarmed by the idea of choking with the foul stuff, even being asphyxiated by it, yet he does not actually visualize it. The thing is still very remote. For after all — he lives in Ealing, which is a long way from Piccadilly or Whitehall. And surely, a gas bomb dropped in Whitehall would not spread all the five miles to Ealing? And anyway haven't we got an air force? How do we know that the damned Huns (or the damned French or the damned Russians or whoever our next 'enemies' may be) — how do we know they'd ever get through at all?

To which the simple answer is 'the damned English got through, in very considerable quantities, during the most exhaustive aerial tests that have ever been made.' Time and again they got through. And they proved, beyond a shadow of doubt, that *no great city can be defended against air attack.*

In the most recent Defence of London Air Manœuvres, out of a total of 250 aeroplanes which took part in a night attack on London, only *sixteen* were even discovered by searchlights, let alone shot down. And it must be remembered that even this meagre proportion was arrived at when the defensive parties were on the alert and prepared for any emergency.

Even if the defensive forces of London were trebled, i.e. even if one in every five of an attacking air force were brought to the ground, what hope would the population of London have? If the hostile air fleet consisted of only 250 aeroplanes, 200 aeroplanes would be left free to carry on their work of destruction.

Professor Haldane says that 1000 aeroplanes would be needed to cause a really efficient holocaust. Nearly every other expert puts the number at 100, or lower. And this is an occasion where I find myself reluctantly on the side of the big battalions.

There is a mass of expert corroboration on my desk

at this moment.[1] Turning up the first report my hand touches, I find a statement by the Earl of Halsbury, K.C., who was formerly Assistant Inspector of High Explosives, and who has made a study of modern gas warfare. Here it is:

'*Mustard gas is the most deadly of known gases. In an area, say, Richmond to Barking, and from Finchley to Streatham, an effective lethal dose would be only forty-two tons. In twelve hours every man woman and child in that area might fail to live.*'

Since one R.A.F. bomber can now carry two tons of bombs, twenty planes could do this work very easily.

More evidence? Very well. It was recently stated by General Crozier in *The Times*, that:

'*During the Great War* 380 *tons of bombs were dropped in and around London. That quantity could now be delivered in less than* 12 *hours.*'

That statement has never been effectively challenged.

Still more? Certainly. We can give you a whole pile of it, if you are still sceptical. Here is a French opinion:

'*With regard to the effects on Paris,* L'Oeuvre *states that the city would have been destroyed, and the famous professor of physics, Professor Langevin stated with regard to the results of these manœuvres that* 100 *aeroplanes, each carrying a ton of gas, could cover Paris with a gas cloud twenty metres thick. This could be done in an hour, and if there were no wind Paris would be annihilated.*'

[1] Those interested in this subject will find all the evidence they need in *What Will Be The Character of a New War?* It is a book to which I gratefully acknowledge my indebtedness. It is published by Gollancz at 5s.

And here is a German assertion, from Siegert, an inspector of the German Air Fleet:

'*A few aeroplanes will be able to reduce the capital of any great state to ashes.*'

And here is an American view, from the late Thomas A. Edison,[1] whose opinion may possibly be of as much value as that of Professor Haldane. (It should also be remembered that since Edison's death, the attacking powers of aircraft have been enormously developed, while defensive measures have stood still.) Edison said:

'*Neither I nor anybody of my acquaintance has discovered any protection against the aeroplane even in its present state of development. There is in existence no means of preventing an aeroplane flotilla flying over London to-morrow and spreading over the millions of Londoners a gas which would asphyxiate those millions in a relatively short time. From twenty to fifty aeroplanes would be amply sufficient for this purpose.*'

He observed (with a smile, according to the interviewer) that with the aid of '*Lewisite*', *the most deadly poison gas yet produced, London's population could be choked to death in three hours.*

However in case you distrust the opinions of amateurs like Edison, it may be advisable to quote General Bradner, Chief Research officer of the Chemical Warfare Service of the American Army. He said, as long ago as 1921. . . .

'*The Chemical Warfare Service has discovered a liquid approximately three drops of which, when applied to any part of the skin, will cause a man's death . . . One plane carrying two tons of the liquid could cover an area one hundred feet*

[1] Enock. *The Problem of Armaments.*

wide by seven miles long in one trip and could deposit material to kill every man in that area by action on his skin. If the men were not protected by gas masks, which would be the case if the attack were made on a city, the fatal area would be several times as great . . . The only limit to the quantity of the liquid which could be made is the amount of available electric power, as nearly every nation has practically an unlimited supply of the necessary raw material. It would be entirely possible for this country (U.S.A.) to manufacture several thousand tons per day, provided the necessary plant had been built.'

In the last twelve years, the efficiency both of aircraft and of poison gas has vastly increased. It is a little difficult to obtain entirely accurate information of the ramifications of this industry, which is naturally averse to publicity. But at present it would seem that the most energetic production of poison gas is to be found, strangely enough, in America. 'At Edgewood, a huge poison gas plant has been built, costing £9,000,000. Within its walls are 218 manufacturing buildings, 79 other permanent structures, 21 miles of standard rail track, 7½ miles of narrow gauge track, 15 miles of macadam roads, 11 miles of high tension electrical transmission lines. 1,400 tons of poison gases are kept in stock, and plant capacity is said to be 800 tons poison gas per day — which means that Edgewood could produce in two months more poison gas than the Germans used throughout the war.'[1]

However, England is not far behind. 'At Porton, close to Salisbury, exists the Government Chemical Warfare

[1] *The Menace of Chemical Warfare to Civilian Populations*, by Arthur J. Gillian, General Secretary Chemical Workers Union.

Experimental Station, where the poison gas products from the Government factory at Sutton Oak, St. Helens, Lancs., are tested out under every conceivable condition obtainable in actual physical results of poison gas, experiments must be and are made on living victims, animal and human. Elaborate apparatus has been devised at Porton for these experiments. Each hut or building is a laboratory and death-house in one. Each contains glass fronted chambers surrounded by glass vessels and tubing. Since 1916 to the present day, experiments have been continuously carried out — thousands of animals (horses, cats, rabbits, guinea pigs, rats and mice) have been used and killed by the experiments or have had to be destroyed immediately after.'

The pile of evidence on my desk has hardly been touched. One could write a long book on this section alone, giving quotations from experts in every country, from officers in every air force, chemists in every great city, politicians in every parliament, from men engaged in every form of activity — all stating, as a fact almost too obvious to be commented upon, that no great city can be defended from the air, and that millions of the population will therefore be subjected, in the event of war, to the deadliest gases with which bombs can be filled.[1]

It is now legitimate to hope that the reader will no longer regard this as a remote problem, but will realize that he is as vulnerable to attack as if he were in the front line of the next war.

It will therefore be apposite if we very briefly suggest to him the nature of the gases with which he is most

[1] Ibid.

likely to become personally and painfully acquainted, in the near future. Familiarity may not breed contempt, in these matters, but at least it will enable him to study symptoms with intelligent interest.

V

The chief poisonous gases may be divided into four classes.

The first class is poisonous when breathed through the lungs, but is without effect upon the skin. The most popular of these gases during the war were Chlorine and Phosgene. Many a recruit will remember his passage through dim grey chambers, filled with Chlorine gas, while he stared at a blank wall, breathing through his respirator, and watching the buttons on his tunic turn from gold to green. This class of gas, since it can easily be kept out by respirators, will certainly never be used again. It is as obsolete as the bow and arrow.

The second class of gas which was employed, with effect, in the war, is the Lachrymatory class. This is really only of value in surprise attacks, when troops are either unprovided with respirators or are unable to adjust them in time. This is also presumably obsolete in the battlefield, as it can be kept out by respirators. However, it is highly probable that it will be used in very large quantities on civilian populations, for two reasons. Firstly because it is comparatively 'humane'. It merely causes temporary blindness which lasts for forty-eight hours, and is accompanied by acute pain. It could therefore be employed very early in any war without too greatly outraging the moral susceptibilities of the country which employed it. Secondly, such a gas, though not fatal, would be, to say the least of it, so embarrassing that it might well be decisive. If you can imagine the greater number of the inhabitants of the city of London rendered blind for two days and two nights, you will be likely to agree with this assumption.

The third and fourth classes of gas are those which most concern us. For in the third class come the various poisonous arsenical smokes, such as Lewisite. These smokes were not greatly used in the war. If they had been, it is almost impossible to imagine what would have happened, because even the pro-gas brethren admit that up till now no efficient respirator has been invented to protect against them. Here is a description of the effects of one of these gases: '*The pain in the head is described as like that caused when fresh water gets into the nose when bathing, but infinitely more severe. These symptoms are accompanied by the most appalling mental distress. Some soldiers poisoned by these substances had to be prevented from committing suicide; others temporarily went raving mad, and tried to burrow into the ground to escape imaginary pursuers.*'

The actual effect of some of these arsenical smokes is to dissolve the lung tissues, so that the victim, at last, literally *drowns* in his own blood.

The fourth class of gas is the blistering gas, of which mustard gas is the noblest example. To give some idea of the effect of this gas, if one small drop of the liquid is put on a piece of paper, and left for five minutes on a man's sleeve, the vapour will penetrate his coat and his shirt, and will cause a blister which will last for six weeks.

In addition to its astonishing powers of speed and penetration, mustard gas, if spread on the ground, retains its deadly effects for over a week. It may therefore be supposed that even a hundred of these bombs, dropped on the City of London, might cause a dislocation which would be seriously embarrassing.

It would be a waste of my time and yours to draw imaginary pictures of these horrors at work.

What I *can* do and have done, is to make a first hand investigation of the City of London's present position as regards *defence* against gas. If you read the next chapter, you will find that it is not quite so dull as this, because it is a purely personal investigation of a very vital problem.

Also, if you remember the original form of this book, you will realize that the next chapter is really the beginning of Part II. For here, we end our little investigation of the preparations for attack, and concern ourselves, for a short while, with the preparations for defence. It is my melancholy duty to warn you that in comparison with the destructive efficiency which we have been reporting up to now, the next chapters will reveal an apathy and inefficiency which are, to say the least of it, disturbing.

CHAPTER V

BEHIND THE MASK

It was a grey, dismal afternoon when I set out for the offices of Anti-Gas Ltd.[1] It was the second day of the new year. The sky was heavy with rain unshed, and the wind had a whine in it, as though the last funeral rites of 1932 were still being fulfilled, round the corner.

I went on foot, because there was plenty of time to spare, and also because the factory lay on the other side of the river, and I love crossing the London bridges on these dim and heavy days. I lingered a little on Westminster Bridge, looking down at the river. It seemed to be hurrying more than usual, away from these restricting banks in a fever to get to the open sea. For there was no peace here. The seagulls screamed and swerved, the little tugs puffed and hooted, the trams argued shrilly behind me. There are times when the view from Westminster Bridge is so lovely that it catches the breath — when the city is set in silver and the sky is a shining space. To-day everything was wrong. Wordsworth could not have written even a limerick about it.

I walked on. The stolid mass of the County Hall loomed up on the left — a building as dull as most of the people who work in it, and completely out of character with the grim and earnest little houses of the Westminster Bridge Road. I passed rows of sordid shops, where

[1] A synonym.

one could buy mauve caps for eighteen-pence and made-up bows for a shilling. There were a great many public-houses, that looked like prisons, though I suppose they were sanctuaries to the people who entered them. There was a florist in which a few early hyacinths wilted. There was a confectioner's displaying its wares of faded pink. And at last I came to the window of Anti-Gas Ltd.

I paused and studied it. I doubt if one out of the hundreds of thousands who pass down this busy street have ever thought it worth looking at. For it was so very quiet and discreet . . . in fact, one might have mistaken it for the office of an old-fashioned solicitor. The bottom part of the window was almost opaque and the objects displayed in it were few and dreary. There was a fire-extinguisher, a respiratory apparatus, and some other object I did not recognize. There was, certainly, nothing to make one realize that here, in this comparatively modest building, was housed almost the only means of defence which the citizens of London possess against gas in the next war.

What? What's that . . . you ask? The only means of defence . . . in this little building? What about the army? The air force? Oh . . . to be sure . . . it *was* proved in the last chapter, pretty conclusively that in spite of the army, and the air force, no great city can be adequately defended from the air, and therefore from gas attacks. Admitted. But what about gas-masks?

Well, Anti-Gas Ltd. are, as far as I am aware, the only English firm manufacturing gas-masks on any large scale. So that my statement above is, in spite of the imaginary interjections of the disgruntled reader, correct. *In that modest building is housed almost the only means of defence which the citizens of London possess against gas in the next war.*

Let us therefore go inside and see what is being done for our safety.

II

I knocked at a little window marked enquiries. The window flew open and a pleasant-faced youth asked my business. I told him.

'Certainly, Sir. This way please.'

We went up some very narrow stairs, dimly lit. It was all charmingly antique and tranquil. I was shown into a small room looking out on to a backyard. Again the feeling of it being a solicitor's office. But there was one object which dispelled this illusion.

It was a glass case, filled with little dolls, all wearing gas-masks.

'What a very excellent idea!' I thought as I approached this singular exhibit. 'Dolls in gas-masks! A most admirable conception! This is by far the most sensible Christmas present which any mother could possibly give to her child. Apart from the fact that her darlings will learn how to put the masks on quickly and efficiently, they will become accustomed to seeing them on the faces of those they love . . . a very necessary precaution!'

And I thought of thousands of small fingers, in the firelit nurseries of England, deftly slipping miniature gas-masks over the waxen cheeks of their beloved dolls.

Then, as I examined these pigmy figures a little more carefully I saw that they were not really dolls. They were models, for demonstration purposes. And some of them were for protection against coal gases, and things like that. However, they could be easily touched up for war purposes and given to the children. Any mother with any sense *will* do so, at the earliest opportunity.

The door opened, and I was conducted to the office of the gentleman who was to show me over the plant. We will call him Mr. X.

III

Now, let me say at the outset that in reporting the proceedings with Mr. X I have none of the pangs of conscience which assailed me on some other occasions. True I was a spy, but in this case I was not a hostile spy. Anti-Gas Ltd. of which Mr. X was a distinguished and efficient employee, is not an armament factory. It is not a slaughter house, like Armsville. It is an *anti*-armament factory . . . its object, in making gas-masks (apart from making money) is to save life, not to destroy it.

But . . . and it is a big 'but' . . . this firm does bear one great resemblance to an armament factory, because, as I was almost immediately to learn, it does not care whose life it saves. 'Kill anybody you like, as long as you give us the order,' say the armament makers. 'Save anybody you like, as long as you give us the order,' says Anti-Gas Ltd.

Here is a picture which illustrates this point clearly.

As we were passing along the corridor, I saw a vast pile of metal discs. They were an odd shape, like bits of a cocktail shaker, and I asked Mr. X what they were.

'Those are parts of gas-masks,' said Mr. X.

'There seem a great many of them.'

'Yes. There are forty thousand.'

'Really? That's encouraging.'

'Encouraging?' Mr. X raised his eyebrows.

'Well – it's nice to know that there'll be at any rate forty thousand people left in England after the next war.'

'In England?' Mr. X stared at me. 'But those gas-masks are going to *Turkey*!'

We passed on. I glanced back at that great pile of metal. So those masks were going to Turkey, were they? In order, I suppose, that when we are engaged in hostilities in the Near East, the Turks may be adequately protected against British airmen, by British masks . . . and may bring British aeroplanes crashing to the ground with anti-aircraft guns manufactured by the British firm of Armsville? Very interesting. Forty thousand gas-masks going to Turkey! Forty thousand Turks saved to carry on the torch of progress!

These reflections were rudely interrupted because Mr. X came to an abrupt halt. We were face to face with a great array of the masks themselves . . . not the metal fittings, but the face coverings, which are at once so hideously human and yet so far removed from life. There they hung . . . row upon row of them, grim and grey, still and sightless. Their blank faces were turned dead towards me, and their canvas features seemed to droop in dejection and despair. And as I looked, a gleam of watery sunshine filtered through the window, caught the metal rods on which the masks were hanging, and sparkled fitfully. So that there was a glimmer behind those gaping sockets, as though men's eyes were peering through them. I wondered whose eyes would one day peer, at what scenes of desolation?

Then Mr. X spoke again.

'Those,' he said, 'are going to another . . . ahem! . . . foreign government.'

IV

Mr. X was very informative.

'It is possible,' I said to him, 'that London may one day be under a shroud of gas?'

'It is possible . . . to say the least of it.'

'And is it possible to provide every man woman and child with gas-masks?'

'Well. . . .'

He paused. And in that pause I imagined that he was thinking much as I was thinking. For if you ask this question seriously, it answers itself. Think of the babies in the slums — the people in the hospitals — in the lunatic asylums — the transport workers. Think of the vast life of a great city throttled in a gas-mask for twenty-four hours. And not only fighting gas, but fire. Evidently these questions were occurring to Mr. X also for he went off at a tangent. He said brightly:

'We could manufacture forty million gas-masks and retail them at five shillings apiece.'

'Could you really?'

'Oh yes. It would be an economic proposition.'

'But what about you . . . your own family?'

'Ah!' He paused again. 'Well, of course, the first thing I should do would be to make one room in the house absolutely gas-proof.'

'How would you do that?'

And now for the moment, I am going to leave Mr. X, in case this conversation sounds too fantastic. For there is a constant danger that this book, which is entirely concerned with facts, may, by its cumulative effect, read like a fairy story. Let us, therefore, remind ourselves of the factual basis of this narrative, and also gain a little encouragement, by quoting from the British Red Cross Society's recent 'First Aid in Chemical Warfare', which is partly based on the official publications of the Army Council.

'*Any room with sound walls, roof and floor, can be rendered gas-proof. The windows, if they do not fit tightly, should be puttied, and all other openings, including the chimney, should be stopped; while the doors should have strips of cloth nailed round them to prevent the entrance of poisoned air. When the room is to be used as a gas-proof shelter, fires and other means of heating should be extinguished as they help to draw in air from outside.*'

This sounds very easy and pleasant. Actually of course, it is not worth the paper it is written on, unless you are able to convince yourself that the population of a vast city would be able to sit indoors, as though they were just shutting out a London fog, for days on end.

We had better get back to Mr. X.

'You would like to see how we test the gas-masks?'

'Very much indeed.'

We dived down some steep wooden stairs, hurried along a corridor, passed through a grey room filled with grey men doing grey things, and emerged into a backyard of peculiar squalor. An acrid odour hung about this yard. It was open to the sky — such sky as there was — and if one looked up, there were tattered clouds, like pieces of old newspaper, blown across a heaven that was curiously like a backyard itself. But there was no particular reason to look up, because here, straight ahead, was an object of grim and compelling interest.

It was a black iron cell, large enough to hold a dozen men, and it had three glass windows wet with moisture. In the base of it, about three feet from the ground, were vent holes which were, at this moment, stuffed with corks. There hovered round this iron monstrosity a smell indescribably disgusting — a smell that was dead, and yet alive, a smell that was despairing and yet had a foul tickle about it. Like a twitching corpse.

While I was gazing at this thing I heard a cough behind me. I looked round and I saw three men, lined up for inspection. Two of them, who were middle-aged, had rather elaborate contraptions round their middles . . . oxygen masks, I believe, which are used for tunnelling parties. The other member of the party was only about nineteen. He was the one who had coughed, and he carried the standardized gas-mask which is supplied to the War Office.

It was this young man who attracted my attention.

He was trembling all over. Why? It was not cold. The air was mild enough. What was the matter with him? He seemed to be about to say something, to cry out. But he did not get the chance, because my guide flicked his fingers, and said:

'All right. Put 'em on.'

Whereupon the men put on their gas-masks. The young man's hands were trembling so much that he could hardly get the straps over his ears.

A man in a white coat opened the door of the cell, went inside, and lit a fuse. A few sparks spat out from the darkness. He came hurrying out again. In a moment fumes and coils of sullen yellow gas began to pour through the open door. We stepped back, quickly.

The guide held up his hand.

'All right. In you go.'

The men stumbled in, like pigs going to a slaughter chamber. The door slammed on them. We went round to the side and looked through the steamy windows . . . I could just discern three grotesque figures, standing like ghosts in the curling fumes.

'Not a particularly lethal gas,' said my companion, pleasantly . . . 'though of course, a good gulp of it would lay you out pretty quickly. Still, it's the psychological effect which is important. We have to *accustom* men to get used to wearing these things.'

I thought of the psychological effect which I had seen in the trembling hands of the young man with fair hair who was shut up in that chamber now. 'Thank you,' I said. 'I quite understand. May they come out now?'

The door was opened. The figures stumbled out. They

removed their masks. The young man's face was dead white. I went up to him.

'Could I borrow your mask?'

'Do you want to go in?'

'Yes — just to see the psychological effect.'

'Certainly.'

Yet, he looked a little doubtful.

'There's not the faintest danger, is there?'

'None whatever. I was merely thinking about your clothes . . . they may smell rather. . . .'

I told him that I did not mind about the smell of my clothes. I took the mask from the young man. It was sweaty inside, and I had to wipe it with a handkerchief.

I put it on. First the strap round the waist, then the chin, then the head, then the whole face piece. As soon as it was on, there was a sense of the world being far, far away . . . shut out. One's breath came in a sort of long wail, and exuded in a hoarse gasp. Wail, gasp, wail, gasp.

'Ready?'

I nodded. I walked up the stairs. Into the chamber. The world, now, was only a whirling of grey veils, a choking and a gasping, a foul nightmare. It was not that one was afraid, for there was nothing whatever to be afraid of. The mask was working perfectly, and even if it had been leaking, a few gulps of this gas would only have been painful, not fatal. No . . . it was the psychological effect (to quote my friend) which was so appalling. One felt so helpless, like a trussed animal in a burning building. And those veils, those grey whirling veils, what if they had been really deadly, if they had been charged with acids which wormed their way through one's clothes, burning, eating away like cancer?

I had had quite enough. I stepped outside. I took off the mask and breathed deeply. Never had air tasted sweeter than in that dirty backyard.

'Funny feeling the first time, isn't it?'

'Very funny.'

'Still it's surprising how quickly you get used to it. Why, a man can wear this mask for twenty-four hours if necessary. Sleep in it, in fact.'

'I know. A woman too, of course.'

'Of course. And they may have to.'

Now will you please stop reading for a moment, and do a little mental exercise. It is a very simple exercise. You know what a gas-mask looks like. Well, just picture, for a moment, a mask on the face of some woman you love. Imagine it, for example, shoved over your mother's head. It will rumple her hair, and the straps will cut into her chin, but, of course, you can't worry about details like that. When she has it on she won't be able to talk to you nor you to her, for you will be wearing a mask too. You will have to sit, silently, gasping. If she has a weak heart — as my mother has — I fear she will not gasp for long. She will suddenly crumple up, and the face you have always loved, that one day you had thought to kiss, in its last stillness, will be kissed and crumpled by the mask. And if you tear it off, it will be stained and pock-marked by the encroaching acid, as she lies on the floor. But if she is a strong woman, she may survive, though I think many women would become insane, under such an ordeal. Even if they were asked to do this, in peace, for practice, they would find, at the end of a few hours, that their brains could not stand it any longer. Twenty-four hours is a long time. Supposing the raid came at four o'clock in the morning. By four o'clock on the following afternoon, you would be wanting your tea, to say the least of it. Your head would be bursting, your brain on fire. . . .

Enough of this. The trouble about all these arguments is that they are so strong, so utterly overwhelming to anybody possessed of the least imagination, that it is difficult to avoid writing at the top of one's voice. Just as it is difficult, in an argument with a militarist, to avoid giving him a sock in the jaw before one has been talking for five minutes. Which is not as illogical as it sounds.

CHAPTER VI

THE YOUNG IDEA

THE scene now shifts to Marlborough College.

We are still occupied with problems of *defence*, and the O.T.C.s, as we are constantly assured by headmasters, are purely defensive institutions. Let us therefore see one at work.

Marlborough College is a rambling cluster of red brick buildings nestling in the shadow of the Wiltshire downs. It accommodates about seven hundred boys, is famous for its old Saxon mound, and has a beautiful chapel with windows by William Morris. It is also famous for its tradition of muscular Christianity, as exemplified in the present Bishop of London, himself an old Marlburian. Its school motto is pleasantly vague — *Virtute Studio Ludo* — and it was in the shadow of this motto that I myself was brought up. I often wished that the masters would occasionally give the *ludo* a rest and pay a little more attention to the *studio*. However, one emerged healthy and cheerful — which is about as much as one can say for the results of most varieties of modern education. And Marlborough turns out fine men, whatever one may say against the system.

I am not one who speaks in a husky voice about his old school, who keeps his old school tie in a sacred drawer. Nor do I annually present myself at reunion dinners to eat luke-warm cod in the company of young men who slap each other on the back and talk about 'old Tomkins'. But I have no sympathy with people who blackguard their old schools merely because it is fashionable to do so. If a man thinks his school did him harm, his duty is to try to change the school. That is what I am trying to do.

The only reason why I returned to my old school, on the coldest day since 1848, was a purely practical one. I wanted to see, with the eyes of maturity, exactly what was being done in the O.T.C. I wanted those three letters, O.T.C., to mean something definite to me, because, at the moment, they only gave me a hazy recollection of hot afternoons in tight uniform, of drill sergeants with purple faces, of clicking heels, and rifles that made one's shoulders sore. And of course, an enormous amount of obscene language while we were firing. You must remember that when I was at school 'there was a war on', and it was the fashion among the boys to apply to the Germans every foul adjective which they had ever heard. And so, whether we were firing at targets or merely letting off blank into the nearest gorse-bush, the running fire of commentary would have put any bargee to shame.

Here we are, then, at Marlborough College. Or rather, overlooking it, for I had motored down from London, and had paused on the hill at the edge of Savernake forest for a moment's sentimental retrospect. Far away, on the other side of the valley, were the bleak downs, over which we had run so many times in the teeth of the winter winds. Down in the valley the little red town was huddled, with its immensely wide High Street, its chapel over which the rooks were perpetually vocal, and its playing fields dotted with white goal posts. And here behind me was the forest, which had been my only true home, my only true love, in those days of early storm. I looked back at it. How familiar were those great avenues of ancient beech, through which the stags still strayed, and in whose metalled branches the wind played the same old tunes!

One tree in particular I stared at, long and curiously. It was under this tree that I had once lain, shivering, while the November leaves whirled about me, and the unheeded rain pattered down on to the thick moss. I was not alone, then. There was another boy beside me. He was wearing the uniform of a second lieutenant, and from time to time he tugged nervously at his belt, and whistled a tune, to keep his spirits up. He was about two years older than I was. He had come down to say good-bye, and I had broken bounds to have this last walk with him.

The walk was finished. He had to catch his train. We lay down under the beech tree for a last look at the old school. He stared out over the valley, and then he said, very quietly, 'Well . . . there's one thing I'm thankful for — when this war's over, there'll never be another. You'll never be dragged into a bloody business like this. Nor any of the kids down there.'

Six weeks later, his skull was blown off. That was in January, 1917.

I took a last look at the old beech tree, got into the car, and sped down the hill. As I drew up at the College gates I heard a sound of shouting and marching. I walked through the gates, and paused.

The Courtyard was filled with boys. The whole school was out, drilling.

'Form fours!'

'Form two deep!'

'Company – pre-sent Arms!'

Through the cold, keen air came the sound of seven hundred young hands striking seven hundred rifles.

They drilled beautifully.

It was quite like old times.

II

I had an appointment with the Headmaster and the Corps Commander.

The Headmaster of Marlborough is a man one instinctively likes and trusts. He is a fine scholar, and he had a distinguished war record. He also has a sense of humour. The Corps Commander is a fine fellow too. I remembered him well, and I hoped that somehow or other, from the conversation we were going to have, something definite would emerge.

However, nothing definite emerged. We sat in a charming chintzy room, fragrant with the scent of freesias, and we talked at cross-purposes. Most of the conversation was not worth recording. But a few curious facts stand out in my memory.

The first fact was that the corps was a completely antiquarian institution. As far as its activities were concerned the last war might never have occurred. I asked the Corps Commander:

'Do the War Office supply you with gas-masks or do you have to buy them yourselves?'

'*Gas*-masks?' He looked quite surprised. 'We don't have any gas-masks! Nor any gas training.'

'*What?*'

'Certainly not!'

I changed the subject.

'And anti-aircraft practice — or whatever you call it — how do you manage about that?'

'I don't understand.'

'But surely it's fairly generally admitted that the next war will be decided in the air?'

'It is not admitted *here*.'

Rebuked!

'Then I suppose you still adopt the general principles of *Infantry Training*, as published by the War Office?'

'Yes.'

Here I would suggest that every parent who wishes to keep in touch with the world, as his boy is being taught to regard it, should buy this book *Infantry Training*, especially Volume 2. It only costs fifteen pence, but it is worth it. It brings back a vanished age. The flash of the bayonet gleams through each of its turgid pages. The shadow of a barbed-wire fence falls across its tersest paragraphs. Anybody who fought in the Boer War would feel thoroughly at home in it, with its chapters on 'fighting in villages', its pretty little suggestions for laying bridges, and its constantly reiterated bombast about 'inculcating the offensive spirit'. Somewhere, hidden away in its 260 pages you will find five modest pages devoted to 'Protection from Aircraft'. You will also find exactly four lines devoted to the subject of gas. Exactly four lines.

To our conversation again. Perhaps the Headmaster saw what was going through my mind, for he said:

'The Corps gives the boys something which they cannot get in any other branch of the school's activities.'

'What does it give them?'

'Discipline. The habit of command.'

'But not the war spirit?'

'Certainly not. That is a thing which I find difficult to explain to enthusiasts in the cause of peace who come down to see me, from time to time. They either come from the League of Nations or from independent organizations. Sometimes they are foreigners. They say to me "you tell us that you are completely pacific and yet you run this officers training corps, which is a military institution. How do you explain that?" I admit that it is exceedingly difficult to explain, to a foreigner. If you tell him that the ideal we have in mind is more Platonic than Prussian, he simply does not believe you.'

Well, I believe the Headmaster. I believe in his complete sincerity. I believe the ideal *is* more Platonic than Prussian. And for that very reason I consider it more poisonous.

I consider it poisonous because, in this matter, I am a realist. When I see a rifle I see something which is designed for one purpose and only one purpose — to kill. To propel a bullet into the heart, lungs, eyes or any other portion of the anatomy you may choose, with fatal results. A rifle, to me, is not a pretty piece of wood and steel, a jolly thing to toss over a boy's shoulder on a summer afternoon, a hearty emblem of patriotism. It is simply and solely a method of killing.

The same argument applies to drilling. When I see boys forming fours, forming two deep, sloping arms, ordering arms, presenting arms, and going through all those revoltingly barbaric exercises which, one had hoped, had been banished from the world for ever, I do not clap my hands with glee and say 'What fun! How good for the little chaps! Playing at soldiers, making *men*!' I am merely filled with profound despair. Because, behind all these pretty manœuvres, behind every military gesture which these boys are making, I see the *object* of it all, which my Headmaster calls Platonic, but which is really true-blue Prussian.

If you doubt that, you can soon dispel your doubts by buying the War Office booklet on O.T.C.s. Turn to the section devoted to the Annual Camp. What is the main object of these camps? According to the War Office, '*to arouse interest in military matters, and thus encourage cadets to take commissions in the supplementary reserve or territorial army*'. Turn through its pages, with their insistence on the importance of getting boys throroughly accustomed to the sight of tanks, 18-pounders, 4.5 howitzers, and other such boyish toys. Revel, if you will, in the collection of army forms it publishes, in its shrill note of discipline, its thinly disguised brutality.

And then ask yourself if you can honestly call the spirit of the corps 'Platonic!'

III

We are now in a position to state, very clearly, the main argument against the O.T.C.s.

That argument is that they are military institutions whose commanders refuse to admit that they are military institutions. In other words, that they keep alive a war spirit, without teaching the boys anything about the practice of modern warfare.

I suggest that the Corps should either be abolished altogether, or should be brought up to date, equipped with gas-masks, instructed in anti-aircraft defence, and clearly and unmistakably instructed in all the horrors of war as it is to-day.

In case this point is not quite obvious, I shall take the liberty of making a few extracts from a letter which the Corps Commander wrote me a few days after my visit to the school. I had written to him to make sure of a few points which had escaped me. Here is his reply:

'*There is nothing to conceal about the O.T.C.*'

'In pre-war days the O.T.C. was about three-quarters of the school. In war days I suppose it was compulsory. It is not compulsory now, *though very few do not join, only about half a dozen.*'

'The War Office gives us £1 a boy who attends his drills, and also passes Certificate A.'

'The Government lend us rifles for which we are responsible.'

'Markmanship is encouraged *but nothing in the way of figures, etc., are used.*'

'There is no question that the War Office considers the O.T.C.s are valuable to provide a reserve of officers in the case of war.'

These are extracts from an honest and straightforward letter. But I do not consider that the state of affairs which it discloses is either honest or straightforward.

Consider the phrase 'it is not compulsory now, though very few do not join, only about half a dozen'. What does that really mean? You may say that the corps is not 'compulsory', but the fact that ninety-nine out of a hundred boys join an institution which most of them heartily detest indicates something very like compulsion.

What actually happens to a boy who decides not to join the corps? He is sneered at, kicked, ostracised, called a 'sissy'. The fact that the sneerers and the kickers secretly envy him only adds extra venom to their persecution. And who is responsible for this attitude? I suppose you can shelve the responsibility on to that vague collection of prejudices which are usually lumped together under the general title of 'the public school spirit'. But who creates this spirit, if not the masters? And how, then, can the masters escape responsibility?

Consider, again, the phrase — 'markmanship is encouraged but nothing in the way of figures are used.' In heaven's name why are not figures used? *Are the boys learning to shoot partridges?* Is it all a pleasant little dream? If you consider it advisable to put these weapons into young boys' hands at all, is it not, to say the least of it, dishonest to disguise from them the true object of these weapons? If ever there was a case where 'figures', of the most gruesomely realistic nature, should be used, it is in a school O.T.C. And after every parade I should suggest that the boys were led through a hall in which a few photographs of wounded were hanging — the sort of photographs which show men with their chins blown off and the top part of the skull missing.

Pacifists are often accused of being illogical. But nothing could ever equal the grotesquely illogical nature of a system which teaches its boys to aim, but discreetly veils from them the objects they are aiming at.

The final phrase of the letter brings me back to my main accusation. 'There is no question that the War Office considers the O.T.C.s are valuable to provide a reserve of officers in the case of war.'

Indeed! And for this reason, we are to suppose, it encourages the youth of England to exercise themselves in manœuvres which bear less relation to modern warfare than the antics of the back row of a charity pageant! For this reason it spends £100,000 a year on keeping from the youth of this country any suggestion of the word *gas!* For this reason, to 'provide a reserve of officers', it teaches them to stand in rows, and gaze down antiquated rifles at meaningless targets, in the vague idea that somehow or other they are doing something gallant, and being of service to their king and country!

If the O.T.C.s are 'valuable to provide a reserve of officers', it is high time they ceased this hypocrisy and came out into the open as military institutions. At the risk of seeming wearisome I really must emphasize the alternative . . . either the corps is a military institution or it is not. You really cannot escape from it. You cannot go shuffling about between your two stools *ad infinitum*. And if it is a military institution, as by now you may be inclined to admit, you must open your eyes and prepare to be honest enough to grant that it is an institution which is, or should be, primarily devised for *killing*, and that if you allow your boy to join it, this is what you are encouraging him to do. The object of an army on active service is to kill as many enemy soldiers as possible, in the shortest time, with a minimum expenditure of the tax-payers' money. The object of an O.T.C., therefore, should be to teach boys to kill other boys. If it does not do this it is a mere waste of time. It would be far better if the boys took off their heavy tunics, with the tight collars, and the puttees that are the best recipe for varicose veins yet invented, and did a little Morris dancing.

CHAPTER VII

THANK GOD WE'VE GOT A NAVY

THE impudence of what I am about to write, in this chapter, is astounding, even to me. I hardly know starboard from port, or stern from bow, and my natural inclination is to call a ship 'it', instead of 'she'. I approach the whole problem of the navy, as a means of defence, not with an open mind, but with a blank one.

Perhaps I should say 'approached', because my mind is not quite as blank as it was. It was very evident, when I was trying to get to the bottom of this problem of defence that I should have to face the little matter of the British Navy. Was it our defence and shield, or was it a white elephant? In a great war, would it protect our people, and ensure our food supplies, as it had always done in the past, or would half of it be blown to smithereens by aircraft while the other half was sunk by submarines?

You may tell me that such questions can only be answered by experts. Maybe. But that is no reason why an enquiring layman should not spend a few months trying to answer them. After all, he is a tax-payer, and the navy costs him quite a lot of money. He has to foot the bill, and there is surely no harm in learning what he is paying for? The Admiralty may tell him that it is none of his business, of course. But the modern tax-payer has no use for that sort of obscurantism. He will be more inclined to sympathize with my own attitude, which made me determine not to be bluffed by the experts, nor blinded by the veils of mystery in which naval matters are always shrouded. After all, at school and in the university one is expected to form intelligent opinions on naval engagements whose importance is purely academic, with data far less voluminous than we possess concerning our own navy to-day, whose importance can hardly be overrated, if one is a citizen of this far-flung Empire.

And so I began to scour the libraries for histories of the navy in the Great War, for forecasts of the navy in the next great war, for warnings, judgments, statistics and what-not. There was a mass of material to read, and it was not till after some months study that I was even able to divide the problem into its main divisions. But it emerged, clearly, at length that the first subject on which the intelligent layman must make up his mind is the power of submarines.

II

There is a school of thought which maintains with considerable force that the development of submarine warfare has rendered surface fleets obsolete. And at first sight this school seems to have an almost unanswerable case.

Here is what the prophets of this school proclaim:

'We base our conclusions on the evidence of the last war. In this, the Mistress of the Seas was nearly rendered impotent by German Submarines, although Germany never had more than 175 submarines, of which less than 60 were in action at the same time.'

However, the submarine Jonahs have a good deal more to say than that. They remind us, for example, that since the war, the building of submarines has been feverish, by every nation but Britain, so that at the time of writing the comparative strength of the Great Powers, in this arm, is as follows:

France	...	84
U.S.A.	...	82
Japan	...	63
British Empire		55

But apart from the mere question of numerical strength, there are further menaces to be considered. Remember, Germany's submarines throughout the war were in by no means an ideal position for threatening our maritime communications.

Her submarines were compelled to find their way through narrow, treacherous seas, alive with mines, and scrupulously patrolled. Yet she sank 8,500,000 tons of British shipping, in the face of these immense odds, and with only 57 submarines in simultaneous action!

It was while I was pondering these facts and trying to find out what they meant that I came across a little book called *Paris or The Future of War* by Captain Liddell Hart.[1] He had come by different methods to the same conclusions, and though he is, as he admits, an amateur in naval strategy, he is a brilliant one, and his observations are worth quoting.

'Contrast Germany's geographical position with that of France, the chief submarine power of the immediate future. Her Atlantic bases lie directly opposite the sea

[1] *Paris*, by Captain Liddell Hart. Kegan Paul.

approaches to the British Isles — in an ideal position for submarine action. Of potential significance also is the position of Ireland, an outer breakwater lying across the gateways to Great Britain, for should ever Ireland lend its harbours to an enemy as submarine bases, the odds would be hopeless.'

'Turn again to the Mediterranean, another long and narrow sea channel through which runs our artery with the East, and where our main naval force is now concentrated. Note that our ships, naval or mercantile, must traverse the *length* of this channel, and worse still, have to filter through a tiny hole at each end — the Straits of Gibraltar and the Suez Canal — while midway there is a narrow "waist" between Sicily and Tunis, barely ninety miles across.'

'Then look at the geographical position of Toulon and of the French naval ports on the North African coast, and note how the *radii* of submarine attack intersect the long single line of British sea communication. Is it not obvious that if in a future war any Mediterranean power was numbered among Britain's enemies, her fleet would find it difficult enough to protect itself against submarines, let alone protect merchant convoys and troop transports?'

III

That, in a nutshell, is the case for those naval critics who maintain that the submarine has torn a hole in Britain's naval shield which no power on earth can mend.

It is a startling argument. A frightening argument. At first sight, an unanswerable argument.

And it is utterly false.

This, at least, is the conclusion I have been forced to, after studying the evidence. Remember, I am a pacifist, but I hope I am an honest one. It would have fitted very well into the plan of this book to be able to write a chapter stating sadly that the British navy was useless . . . an obsolete collection of submarine-fodder. However, it does not happen to be true. Because, the evidence all goes to show that the damage done by submarines in the Great War was not due so much to the strength and invincibility of the submarine attack as to the *weakness of the defence against them.*

All that is argued about the relatively small number of German submarines during the Great War and the damage inflicted by them is true. In fact, this part of the argument can be actually strengthened, when one realizes how small a proportion of submarines can be kept in action at one time, owing to the necessity for extensive repairs, both to the ships and to the nerve-racked men.

But . . . and it is a big 'but', as soon as the British Admiralty woke up (after some years of slaughter and appalling loss), it became very evident that the submarine would be beaten. And actually, though most people do not realize this, it *was* beaten, by the Convoy system.

It is quite beyond my powers to give you a technical description of the Convoy system.[1] Its main principle is implicit in its title. It was proved, at the end of the

[1] The interested reader will find plenty of illuminating facts in *The Naval History of the World War*, by Captain Frotheringham.

war, that convoys with escorting craft, carrying guns, ran far less risk than single vessels. How striking was the decrease may be gathered from these facts:

'The fear that Convoy might break down under the conditions of modern warfare was soon dissipated, and none can doubt that the system proved the salvation of the Allies. . . . On May 20th, 1917, the first Convoy reached England from Gibraltar without any loss. It was followed by another, arriving from Hampton Roads, likewise intact. The first assembly numbered 17 ships, and the second 12 . . . by October no fewer than 1502 steamers of 10,656,300 tons d.w. in 99 Convoys had been brought into port, with the loss of only 24 vessels; of these, only 10 had been sunk in Convoy. The remainder were lost either after separating or through the disobedience of their masters. An outstanding feature amongst the results of Convoy was that, *during the last four months of the year, only* 6 *ships were sunk farther out to sea than* 50 *miles, instead of* 175 *vessels similarly destroyed during the period from April to August. Before the introduction of Convoy, ships were being slaughtered at anything up to* 300 *miles out in the Atlantic.*'[1]

One of the results of this system was that the submarine was forced to rely upon the torpedo, which is in itself a far more uncertain weapon of attack than is generally realized.

Let me quote an expert on this point:

'Committed to under-water attack, a submarine's prospect of reaching a torpedo-firing position becomes remote. She has to submerge many miles from her prey

[1] *The German Submarine War*, by R. H. Gibson and Maurice Prendergast. Constable.

to avoid being sighted, and when once submerged, she has relatively poor mobility. If sighted on the surface before diving, her attack can easily be rendered abortive by alterations of course. The inability of submarines, *after Convoy and Group Sailing were instituted*, to locate and successfully attack merchant vessels in the open sea, forced enemy submarines to operate at points of convergence near our coasts where *surface craft* levied a heavy toll.'[1]

However, in addition to Convoy, (which it is to be hoped that the Admiralty would immediately adopt on the outbreak of war), there is also the hydrophone to consider, which makes it possible for submarines to be detected at a great distance under water. A submarine under water, as we have observed, can only travel at a relatively slow speed, so that when detected by means of the hydrophone it is an easy matter for ships to change their course. The seas are so vast that evasion is relatively easy, except at vital points where narrow straits are to be passed, or in the vicinity of ports. But in these places it is not difficult to arrange for a number of small ships, equipped with depth charges and hydrophones, to detect, and if possible, sink the attacking submarine.

I am informed that swift steam trawlers are adequate for this purpose, so that at outbreak of war (or prior to this) a great number of such small vessels could be quickly prepared. True, we must not forget the possibility of inventing noiseless engines to evade the hydrophones, but at the moment this has not been done, and therefore it is an invention which cannot be definitely taken into consideration.

It would be foolish to ignore the submarine menace

[1] *The Great Delusion*, by 'Neon'. Ernest Benn Limited.

entirely . . . to deny, for example, that British trade in Mediterranean waters would be in danger. But we must not *overestimate* the dangers by misreading the lessons of the World War. That is all I am pleading for. We must not consider the geographical position alone. And even the geographical position is not so important as the Liddell Hart school maintains, since the submarine can keep out to sea for long periods when once clear of the harbours. So that the handicap in the case of Germany was not so great as he makes out.

Summing up this section of the argument – (and you will not forget that I humbly admitted my impudence and ignorance at the beginning of the chapter) – it seems to me that the intelligent layman, if he goes direct to his sources, will arrive at the conclusion that though the British Navy may be endangered by the submarine, the danger is by no means likely to be mortal.

IV

Now let us consider the next batch of naval Jonahs – the school which maintains that navies can be blown to smithereens from the air.

I need hardly remind the reader that this is a school of thought which made an instant appeal to me. Being of an imaginative and highly strung nature, inclined to rush my fences, I approached this problem, at the outset, with very definite and very highly coloured prejudices. It would be positively painful to describe how these prejudices were shattered, one by one, remorselessly, by the cold bombardment of facts with which the experts presented me.

These facts boil down to one — that bombardment from the air on to moving objects at sea is, and must always be, a game of chance, in which the difference between success and failure is determined only by a fluke or a series of flukes. And the reason for this uncertainty is inherent in the unchangeable nature of the elements.[1]

We may sum it up as follows:

1. The pilot has no sure means of gauging his speed or direction if he is not in sight of some stationary object . . . (unless, of course, he can obtain information by directional wireless, or make astronomical observations — neither of which aids would be available in the heat of battle). This is due to the fact that an aeroplane encounters only such air-resistance as is made by her own engines. Being free from land, or from any stationary objects, she floats in the air element, part and parcel of it. Supposing she has a speed capacity of 100 miles an hour, her flight, as measured by the land below, may be 80 miles an hour, if she is fighting a 20-mile an hour wind, or 120 miles an hour if the wind is behind her. But it is all the same, as far as the pilot can judge. The landsmen may see an aeroplane in a gale and think she is having a thin time of it, 'riding the storm'. This is a landsman's illusion. The pilot does not feel the gale, and can only gauge it very roughly indeed. These are facts which are born out in countless aerial logs.

Therefore, no pilot can ever reach a *certain* position

[1] These arguments are developed at length in 'Neon's' *The Great Delusion*, which seems to me to make out a quite unanswerable case.

from which to aim, as long as the air is the air, and the sea is the sea. He is like a man trying to shoot partridges from a motor car whose speed varies violently at every ten yards.

2. The bomb itself is equally volatile.[1] Most amateurs' knowledge of bombing ships is confined, either to their own imagination, or to the remembrance of one or two films, where a handsome pilot swoops out of the air, with a 'roar' of engines, skims over a deck and drops a bomb which wreaks its deadly work on the wicked captain and the hirsute crew. He does not realize that endless rehearsals were necessary for this conjunction — that even when the stage captain did his utmost to be hit, and manœuvred his vessel, time and again, by megaphone, into the aeroplane's course, and even when the smoke bombs were ready to explode, in case the aeroplane came near enough to 'fake' a hit, there were so many misses that the director swore about the expense of it all.

For we have to remember, as Neon has explained, once and for all, that the fall of a bomb is regulated not only by its own weight and the speed at which the aeroplane is travelling, but by the *angle* of the machine and the strength of the wind. In other words we arrive at the conclusion that a pilot has to juggle with five separate factors:

i. Wind Strength
ii. Altitude
iii. Speed through space

[1] 'Neon' must forgive me if I borrow again, even from memory!

iv. Actual direction relative to target and wind
v. Angle of flight

All these things, remember, in *addition* to anti-aircraft!

Is it therefore to be wondered that so little damage, comparatively, was done to fleets by aircraft during the Great War?[1] And is it to be feared that in the next war they will do so very much more?

These facts do not in any way invalidate the lessons which I have drawn, in preceding chapters, concerning the real menace and horror of aerial bombing of *towns*. For one thing, the argument that an aeroplane cannot determine its position is obviously inapplicable, for the simple reason that the aviator is circling over a fixed object. For another, a hit or a miss is, in the bombardment of a town like London, almost equally valuable. True, the target may be Whitehall, but even if the bomb goes as far afield as Piccadilly Circus, it can hardly be said to have been useless. A certain number of bombs might fall in the Thames or in Hyde Park, but the area covered by water or park-land in London is a very minor proportion of the vast space of crowded streets which remains open for attack. Again, any bomb on land is *infectious*, whereas any bomb at sea is *sterile*, unless it makes a direct hit. By 'infectious' I mean of course that it causes fire which spreads, or gas which is caught in innumerable pockets. A bomb dropped in the water does little damage except to the fishes in the immediate vicinity. I am also informed that there is very little danger from gas at sea, for reasons which seem almost too obvious to enumerate.

[1] 'The aircraft did less in sinking submarines than almost any other weapon.' Commander Bellairs in a debate on the Air Estimates.

V

We now come to the third scare of the naval Jonahs — Japan. This is really the only other navy, apart from that of the U.S.A., which we need fear *singly*. A war between the U.S.A. and the British Empire is not unthinkable, it is true — nothing is unthinkable in the hideous state of world politics — but it is happily more remote. And it might, in my opinion, be actually less appalling a world-prospect than war between the British Empire and Japan — partly because of the comparative level-headedness of *both* parties to the dispute, but principally because of the chaos which an Anglo-Japanese war would cause in the East. It is to the East that our eyes instinctively wander when we consider this question. And as our eyes wander there, they rest at once on Singapore.

It is not my intention to enter the already crowded lists of those who argue concerning the respective merits of Singapore and Hong Kong as naval bases. It is enough for the average layman to look up these places on the map, and to realize their relative positions with regard, not only to Japan, but to Australia. Australia is the forbidden paradise which the Japanese covet.

Well, what happens to the British navy if the Japanese pick a quarrel in, let us say, the internal affairs of China, and declare war on England, when our fleet is 12,000 miles away? For a very ingenious and illuminating answer to this question the reader would do well to study a book called *Navies of To-day and To-morrow*, by Captain Bernard Ackworth. Captain Ackworth taught me more about the naval aspect of the next war than any of the other prophets. He may be wrong, or officially discredited, for all I know, but at least it seems difficult to pick a hole in the following argument.

Japan would naturally choose a moment for declaring war when the British fleet is in the Mediterranean. Her first objective would certainly be Hong Kong. Those who imagine that she would begin by attacking Australia, thousands of miles from her bases (a continent requiring vast forces to hold), underrate the Japanese intelligence as gravely as those who maintain that she would attack Singapore. Why should she go 3,000 miles to a highly fortified base of minor importance when she need go only 1,000 miles to a comparatively meagrely fortified base of supreme importance?

Assuming then that Hong Kong is attacked and falls, as it well might, long before the British fleet has time to reach it, Japan would have no great difficulty in fortifying it, and holding it, even if she decided to withdraw her main fleet to her home waters. The British, on the other hand, would be faced with appalling difficulties in their endeavour to recapture Hong Kong. They would, in fact, be faced with a long war, of uncertain issue, and gigantic cost, for in the meantime Japanese cruisers would be in a position to devastate our trade throughout the Far East.

It would need half a book to develop these arguments at full length. If I developed them, I could probably be sued for breach of copyright. If I skimped them, I should be doing the Ackworth school an injustice. I will therefore leave them and ask you to study this book yourself.

However, there is one reflection here, arising out of these points, which I cannot refrain from publishing. It is this, that the more one studies British naval policy, the more one is struck by the almost unbelievable *waste* which results from the Admiralty's decisions. I said that I had no intention of entering the lists of those who argue concerning the merits of Singapore. But unless these things are so unutterably mysterious to the layman that black looks white, and vice versa, it would seem that Singapore was one of the costliest and most obvious mistakes which we have ever made. I believe the Admiralty officials realize this, by now, but will not admit it.[1]

Is it too much to suggest that possibly the cheerful sound of grinding axes may echo even down the immaculate corridors of the British and Japanese Admiralties?

We can now leave this section of our examination, with the feeling that though the British navy is by no means in danger of immediate extinction, even in a struggle with our most powerful naval rival, yet the odds

[1] With regard to Hong Kong as a base, I am not forgetting that this has its disadvantages. The recent policy has been constantly to increase the size of battleships, and to add what is known as the 'bulge' to them, which is planned as protection against torpedo action. 'The 'bulge' battleships are unable to be repaired or refitted in Hong Kong, in fact in most naval bases commanded by Britain, because they are too large to enter the docks which were previously built. Thus, if a ship sustains serious damages, it means that she must be able to stand the 3,000 miles journey to Singapore or go under. This, of course, refers only to the largest size battleships. Hong Kong could be used as a base for cruisers, destroyers and submarines. But not the large battleships. However, this disadvantage could, in the event of war, be overcome by removing the floating dock stationed at Singapore to Hong Kong. This dock is capable of taking the largest battleships.

are not so strongly in our favour as to justify complete confidence.

In the next and last section, our confidence will be still more gravely shaken.

VI

Here is the reason for our fears. A very simple table of statistics, at which we can glance, remembering that the British navy runs on oil, and not coal.

The world production of petroleum is as follows:[1]

United States	845,803
Russia	157,000
Venezuela	116,100
Rumania	47,000
Persia	45,500
Dutch East Indies	39,000
Mexico	34,000
Colombia	16,790
Peru	11,500
Argentina	10,000
Poland	4,400
Japan	2,000
Ecuador	1,700
Germany	1,200
Iraq	800
Other countries	900
	1,333,693

[1] See *Statesman's Year Book* for 1932. Figures represent 1000 barrels.

British Empire	
Trinidad	10,000
India	8,000
Sarawak	5,000
Egypt	1,800
Canada	1,700
	26,500

Those figures are, to say the least of it, illuminating. The interested reader, who cares to play with the idea of war with America, will note that America controls roughly 76 per cent of the world's oil production as compared with our $1\frac{1}{5}$ per cent.

You can't run oil-burning warships without oil any more than you can sail trawlers without sails. The idea of the complete immobility of the British navy in the event of war with America (or in the event merely of a hostile America), is so strange and fantastic that the layman finds it difficult to grasp. Yet it *must* be grasped. And it seems to me, in essence, as sinister as any of the wild imaginings with which I began this chapter, as lurid as any 'H. G. Wells fantasy' of a vast battle-fleet being bombed out of existence by an air-fleet.

'Does not such a position place our friends in America in a position to dictate our naval policy, and indeed forcibly to keep, or to break, the peace of the world, for all countries, except America, are now dependent on foreigners for the movement of their ships? Here is a bondage indeed for the necessarily greatest sea-power! No words, no Kellogg Pact, no sentiment, no sophistry can alter the indisputable fact of our present bondage!'[1]

It may be a staunch Imperialist who wrote those words, but they are very obviously capable of adaptation to my pacifist argument that this country may be navally indefensible in the event of war. For it is an acknowledged fact, in the Admiralty, that the British Navy is no longer in a position to engage in any lengthy conflict, unless supplied by America.[2] *The oil supply under British command would only last six weeks at the outside.*

Oil seems a small detail, when you think of the vast organization of the British navy. But then, we are living in a mechanical age, where details are of vital importance. A single defective screw may bring destruction to a great machine and death to multitudes.

One hears vague rumours that an adequate supply of oil can now be obtained from coal. If these rumours are correct, we can still thank God we have a navy, although a sudden immense consumption of coal for naval purposes would obviously play havoc with our industrial life. If they are incorrect, we have not much to be thankful for.

[1] Ackworth.

[2] A friend who read this chapter observed to me that the obvious moral to be drawn from it was a strong Anglo-American alliance. I remember Mr. Randolph Churchill making the same contention, with considerable energy, at a week-end party–with such energy, in fact, that the only American present went upstairs to lie down. Needless to say I am a passionate believer in Anglo-American friendship and co-operation. But those persons who pin their faith to an exclusive and arbitrary alliance forget that such an alliance would inevitably breed a counter-alliance, and that the world would be faced with a precarious Balance of Power of immense potentialities for evil.

I think it is the duty of the British Admiralty to set our fears at rest.

We therefore end this chapter on a note of interrogation. If our oil supply is assured, we can presumably protect our trade, and repel invasion by sea and land, though obviously we are still vulnerable from the air. If it is not. . . .

VII

It is now necessary to remind the reader, once more, of the original form of this book. That form has been largely shattered, but it may be dimly noticeable that we are now at the end of Part II, which has dealt mainly with methods of *defence*, and their futility.

I should be the last person to claim that I have examined all the evidence. That would be the work of a lifetime, and no student of international affairs who is a preacher as well as a prophet can afford to give to this study his life's endeavour, because he is so convinced of the urgency of the danger that he feels impelled to deliver his message before the flames have broken out.

All the same, I think it may be claimed, firstly, that we have done something to show the power of the offensive arm, and secondly that we have done something to show the weakness of the defensive arm. By steps which may have stumbled, but have at least been honest, we have reached the conclusion that another great war would almost certainly result in the extinction of tens of millions of Europe's civilian population, by gas, by death from the air, by starvation or by disease. We have suggested (not without expert corroboration), that no amount of war 'preparation', short of covering a whole country with a roof of steel, will be of any avail against the Furies that are straining at the leash. We have decided that such futile 'preparations' as we and other nations, are making, are only likely to make it more difficult to hold that leash, are only likely to act as irritants . . . that *nothing* will save civilization, if war breaks out.

To sum up, it is to be hoped that we have exposed the most evil and obscene lie of the world's history. '*Si vis pacem, pare bellum*. . . .' A lie whose utterance should be made a criminal offence in all countries with a pretence to culture, or even to sanity.

It seems a hopeless situation. And it is certainly time that we had a change, and got on to Part III, where we shall see some of the efforts the world is making for peace.

Let us therefore take the first train to Geneva, to the City of Hope, and see what awaits us there.

CHAPTER VIII

THE CITY OF HOPE

'GENEVE!'

I pulled my scarf tighter round my neck, for I had a poisonous cold, edged a little further down the stuffy corridor of the *wagon-lit*, and rubbed my finger on the steamy glass to catch a glimpse of the view. But I was too late. We were already in the station, and all I saw was a flowing platform, and a blurred mass of advertisements for Swiss dentifrices, which suddenly crystallized, as the train stopped, into a row of grinning teeth.

I was in a very bad humour. The night had been insufferable. I had been forced to share my *wagon-lit* with a Swiss gentleman who wore stays and whistled in his sleep. He was already adhering firmly to the lower berth when I got in, at Paris. His stays were shamelessly dangling from a hook on the wall. They made me feel extremely British. I looked at them and at him, registering unutterable contempt. But all he did was to pray that I would ascend, as quickly as possible, to the upper berth, as he was *épuisé*. I undressed, ascended, and tried to sleep. But all the time I was hating the Swiss gentleman, and sending down streams of malicious animal magnetism upon him. Illogical, you say? As a pacifist I must regard the Swiss gentleman as my brother — must love him, stays and all? That is nonsense.

It is precisely because a man is insular that he should be international.

It is precisely because his instincts forbid him to regard the Continental as his brother that he should support institutions which compel him to do so. When I first walked into the hall of the League of Nations I saw so many unpleasant foreigners that I felt that Englishmen were, by comparison, gods. I saw Italians whose faces oozed with grease, Japanese with such fixed and irritating smiles on their faces that I wanted to bash them, Frenchmen who smelt of *violette de parme* and looked as though they had just come from a rather slippery orgy with pink and white mistresses, Spaniards of abominable arrogance, elbowing people about. The only people for whom I felt any real kinship were the Germans and the Americans. I bristled with Britannic zeal. For this very reason, I prayed for greater strength to the League of Nations as a curb on my own brutish instincts.

II

The sun came out as I stepped on to the pavement outside the station, and as it was only a short way to my hotel, I decided to ignore the hotel bus, and walk. Already, over the tumbled roofs, I had caught a glimpse of snow-clad mountains. They looked very lovely, but strangely formal, like white ornaments arranged against a blue wall. Down below, at the end of the street was a glimpse of silver blue water. I walked towards it, past shops that were just opening for the day . . . shops from whose dark interiors came delicious smells of bread fresh from the oven, and fruit, and straw, and hot chocolate.

The lake was adorable — laced with bridges, and alive with birds. Little black coots bobbed up and down on the sharp wavelets, seagulls circled, perpetually screaming, and swans glided majestically backwards and forwards, craning their long necks at the passers by, demanding bread. These birds are, perhaps, the most typical example of Geneva's local colour. Their cries form an eternal accompaniment to all that one says or does. I looked to see if I could find any doves among them, but there did not seem to be any. A regrettable omission, I thought.

Well, I had managed to get a *coup d'oeil* before breakfast . . . a sense of the vast lake, bordered with charming, formal buildings, and a sense of the brooding mountains in the distance . . . so I felt justified in going to the hotel for a cup of coffee. I was strangely excited and elated at really being in Geneva at last. Who knew what odd intrigues, what stirring events, might not be coming to me?

And as soon as I entered the hall of my hotel, the excitement increased. For though it was still early in the morning, there was a bustle of cosmopolitan activity such as one would see in no other hall in the world. A Japanese woman in black was pacing quickly up and down, in the light of the tall windows. She was clutching a little attaché case under her arm as though somebody might seize it from her. Two Greeks argued in the shadow of a palm. A trio of Italians stood in the centre of the hall, performing the usual physical exercises which invariably accompany conversation between persons of this volatile nationality. An extremely fly-blown English clergyman stood in the doorway reading the *Tatler*, upside down. And a French lady, of evidently international reputation, leant back in an arm-chair, talking to a middle-aged compatriot whose veins stood out on his forehead. She talked in an attractive, hoarse voice. I tried to hear what she was saying. But the only word I heard, constantly repeated, was the word *sécurité*. I wondered what it meant. Security? Security? Was she speaking internationally or personally? Security? Was she talking about disarmament? Or was she just being disarming? I looked casually at her ankles, and I sighed. I fear she was just being disarming.

III

After breakfast, I went out again and walked along the Quai. You may be impatient to get to more serious things, but I cannot help that. I can never settle down to work, in a new city, until I have absorbed something of its atmosphere. And in any case, peace or no peace, I cannot resist the temptation of writing about the clock-shops.

For every other shop on this long promenade is a clock-shop. The windows sparkle with clocks of every conceivable colour, size and shape. There are clocks in brilliant enamels, clocks in coarse woods, with brightly painted peasants nodding away the minutes. There are clocks the size of green peas, exquisitely jewelled with tiny emeralds, dangling on a frail chain. There are very modern clocks, with chromium-plated pistons relentlessly jogging up and down. There are terribly arty clocks, showing a picture of cotton-wool mountains with the clock-face painted to look like the setting sun. There are, of course, thousands of cuckoo-clocks, and cow-clocks too, that whirr and moo, and clocks like churches, the simple wooden churches of the mountains above.

Time is *en fête* in these enchanting shops. The passing hour has been turned to a carnival. Is it three or four or five or six? Night or day? What does it matter? The clocks tick on gaily, flicking their tiny figures in perpetual contempt of accuracy. A clock, one had thought, was a sober thing — a guide and mentor. A clock reproved one — was always hinting that it was time to stop, or time to start — was always tut-tutting because one did not obey. A clock, yes, *one* clock. But ten thousand clocks are different. Time seems to have no control over them. They put their little hands to their faces and pull a long nose at him. He runs round, in the person of some tiresome man, trying to pull those hands into their proper place, but they are too many for him. So, at last, Time gives up, and the clocks tell as many stories as they please. And if you go into one of these little shops, and linger for a while, you will hear every hour of the day struck, in sweet tinkling sounds, and gay bells, and ridiculous squeaks. And you feel that the clocks are laughing at Time, who is no longer their master, nor yours.

However, we cannot completely ignore time in this book, so we must get back to business and the hotel.

In the hall a friend was waiting for me. We will call him Mr. A. He is so charming and intelligent a man that he will have to be kept severely in the background, or he will lead us astray, down delightful but unprofitable paths. He is a young man, with a fair pointed beard, an amazingly clear complexion, blue eyes, and a depressing knowledge of European politics.

'Good morning.'

'Good morning.'

'Good journey?'

'Foul.'

'You look exhausted. I think a glass of *champagne nature*, don't you?'

'I *had* thought of a Pernod. . . .'

'Pernod in Geneva is not to be recommended. The *champagne nature* is quite drinkable, at two francs.'

'In that case. . . .'

We ascended to the bar. The *champagne nature* was very drinkable. I asked my friend a question which had been on my lips ever since I met him.

'Have you got tickets for the Disarmament Conference this afternoon?'

He nodded.

'I bet that'll be exciting!'

He looked at me curiously, but made no reply.

We went in to lunch.

IV

But really, you may ask me — what *have* all these things to do with our book? Did we not come to Geneva to see the League of Nations? Why, then, are we dallying like this?

For the simple reason that you, as a reader, are presumably very like me, in that you are easily bored. And never yet have I read anything whatever about the League of Nations which was not unutterably boring. I have never yet read a book which told me what Geneva looked like. I have never had a sense of men meeting over momentous matters in a great city . . . never visualized those men, nor the streets they walked in, nor the sounds they heard, nor the smells they smelt. Geneva has always been a pale ghost, a newspaper abstraction. Its principal figures have talked in paragraphs. The League of Nations, in the eyes of the great British public, and in the eyes of every other great public too, is a bore. Why? Who made it a bore? Why is it that this astonishing city where the ends of the earth are met together receives less *popular* publicity than the latest silly night club in Mayfair?

A new tune, a new lipstick, a new tie that some film star is wearing, a new way of cooking lobster, a new fashion for wearing hair — oh yes — editors will regale their readers, day after day, year after year, with such puerilities. But 'Gossip' and Geneva do not go well together.

Why not? 'Gossip' has a real importance in the world. It is the froth on the surface of the deep, swelling waves — the froth which shows which way the waves are driving. Men will follow that froth, even though they know not where it is leading them. In the present era of universal semi-education, where every man can spell, without knowing the meaning of the words he is spelling, it is vitally important that 'gossip' should be given him about the League of Nations — that he should take an interest in it as a human institution.

Until I went to Geneva I did not even know what sort of building the League of Nations met in. Do you? No? Very well — we will go along and see it. But we had better be prepared for a shock.

V

We walked along the Quai, my friend and I. It was an exquisite afternoon. The lake of Geneva is one of the moodiest stretches of water in the world — it can entreat, dazzle, mystify, depress . . . it can spread itself before you with the enchantment of a pale and magic carpet, and it can stretch itself out like a piece of sullen asphalt. To-day it was ethereally beautiful. Where did air and water meet? And white and blue? The mind agreeably fashions these questions as one walks along, in a dream, and when the mind is thus occupied, the body is ill-directed. Which means that one collides with people.

After one of these collisions — with a cocotte in deep orange make-up — my friend brought me back to earth by telling me that we must cross the road, because we were just approaching the League of Nations building. My heart beat high. We crossed the road. We turned the corner. As we did so, the sun shone full in my eyes, and a sudden gust of wind made me clutch at my hat, so that for a moment I did not quite realize what was in front of me. And then I saw 'it', and I blinked. For in front of me was only a small, dirty hotel.

'But . . . the League of Nations?'

'That's it.'

I blinked again. I still saw only a small dirty hotel. Its date seemed about 1850. It was a greenish-yellow building of, I think, four stories.

'*That?*'

'Certainly. We'll walk round it.'

Dazed, I followed him. We crossed the road. All the time, I stared up at this singularly uninspiring edifice. It seemed utterly impossible that this could house the League of Nations. For although it would not be accurate to say that I had dreamed of a white palace set upon a hill, with doves crooning among groves of myrtle, it would be even more inaccurate to say that I had dreamed of a second-rate hotel in a back street, with a garden containing only a few old Brussels sprouts. After all, one had been given to understand, by the anti-League press, that the League was an institution of almost inconceivable costliness. One had read that the British taxpayer was being bled white to provide for the League's luxurious accommodation. I did not know at the time that the actual cost of the League of Nations to my country was the exact equivalent of the expenditure of half a crown a year to a man with an income of three thousand pounds. I thought vaguely that the League must cost a lot of money, but it was so obviously worth it that I did not worry very much. Therefore, the sight of the League building was saddening.

Particularly sad was the garden, with its sixteen Brussels sprouts. They were so very antique, so decrepit. And there they were, right in the centre of the mangy garden. Couldn't somebody have removed them? Couldn't the Belgian delegate have done so? Or had he, perhaps, planted them there himself, as a gesture?

These reflections were interrupted by my friend.

'That section in front of you was added to accommodate the Disarmament Conference.'

'Oh!'

There was nothing else to say but 'oh'. For this new building before which we had paused looked like a mixture of a garage and a greenhouse. It was made of iron and glass, and whenever there was any paint it was coloured khaki.

'It is very hot in summer,' said my friend.

'And very cold in winter, I expect,' I added politely.

'On the contrary, it is so hot in winter that the English delegation is almost incapacitated.'

Which explained a great deal about the policy of my country which had hitherto been obscure to me.

VI

It was ten minutes to three. The disarmament conference was timed to begin at three, so we went inside.

My heart beat high. The conference had reached a stage of crisis. The reader must remember that I am describing the period immediately prior to Japan's departure from the League, and though that is ancient history, now, there was at that time a tremendous sense of tension in Geneva. Would Japan bow to the moral force of a world arraigned against her? Or would she rattle her sabre in our faces? And if she did, would the League take action, or content itself with scolding? And if the League were unable to take action, would it mean the last 'death-blow' to internationalism?

We walked up some stone steps, presented our tickets, and were ushered into a long gallery that looked down on to the main hall, a large, simple white room, its floor filled with desks on which pens and paper were laid.

Anybody who has ever attended a disarmament conference — and God knows, it looks as though there will be every need of such conferences for a good many years to come — will agree that the first thing that strikes him is the heat. It is appalling. It seems to rise up from the floor below, reach the ceiling, and bound back again in great torrid draughts. And as the hall fills, the heat is accentuated, made doubly uncomfortable by the fumes of tobacco which come from the cheroots, the pipes, the cigars, and the Turkish, Virginian, Brazilian, Egyptian and every other variety of cigarette which is being smoked.

The hall is almost full now. How can men work in this atmosphere? Why, in this haze they can hardly see each other! I am twenty years younger than the average delegate, and I have eaten a light lunch, consisting mostly of salad and water, but already I am half asleep. What must be their condition, after the heavy meals which I have seen them devouring in their hotels? And I fall to thinking of all the acids that must be fermenting in those distinguished stomachs, of the starches warring against the proteins, of the distressed carbo-hydrates and the inadequate pepsins. I think of old hearts wearily pumping the over-sugared blood through hardened arteries, the hearts that have also to fight against choking lungs. And suddenly, I want to stop the conference, and bundle all the delegates, by force, into vans which would take them up on to the mountains, and keep them there on a diet of orange juice for a fortnight before they began to make any more speeches.

These are no wild speculations, unworthy of record. Man is what he eats and drinks and breathes. There is too much eating and drinking and too little breathing at Geneva. I doubt if Geneva errs in this respect any more than any other great political centre. Its record is probably rather better. But even the shortest sojourn at a disarmament conference makes one feel that the world will never know peace until it is run by vegetarians, and until its business is conducted in the open air.

Secret diplomacy has more than a merely symbolical connection with closed doors and barred windows.

VII

And now, back to our Strangers' Gallery, where I have to show you a scene which I should much prefer you not to see. It is a scene which will delight the enemies of the League — a scene that possibly they may quote against me. I will run that risk. Because after all, the whole of this journey which we are making together is a search for the truth.

The truth about the disarmament conference, as I saw it, on that first afternoon, seemed to be exceedingly ugly.

At the beginning, I was too fascinated by the spectacle of all these famous men below me to realize that anything was wrong. I merely watched eagerly. I saw the Aga Khan wandering in, looking extremely amiable, and much tidier than he looks on race-courses. He shook hands with a dozen men before he found his seat. I saw Arthur Henderson, the President, taking off his tortoiseshell glasses and wiping them, over and over again, as though he hoped thereby to see a clear way out of the world's problems. I saw Paul-Boncour, who walked in very quickly, frowning at everybody, and sat down, and buried his head in his hands. They were discussing the French plan for disarmament, this afternoon, and it had a somewhat chilly reception. Other figures I recognized, whom, at one time or other, I had encountered in various parts of Europe . . . General Tanczos, who was lately minister of war to Hungary, Aghnides, a brilliant Greek, a true pacifist, with a brain like a knife, Benes, the late Prime-Minister of Czecho-Slovakia, worldly, urbane, and, as usual, clad in a very badly fitting jacket, Yen, the delegate for China . . . 'the Chinese Demosthenes' they called him . . . sitting alone, staring at the ceiling. And who was that little fat man there, with a pleasant face that looked as if it had been slightly squashed? And why were they all staring at him?

I turned to my friend and asked who he was.

'That is Litvinoff.'

'Litvinoff!'

It was a magic name to me. A very dreadful name in England — implying evil things in the brightest shade of red — a name that had in it an echo of Soviet intrigues, high treason and Lord knows what else. Yet it was also a name associated with the first really superb gesture for Peace which the modern world has ever known, for it was Litvinoff who, a few years ago, was the spokesman of the Soviet plan for total disarmament.

'You want to stop war?' cried Soviet Russia. 'All right — let's abolish all armies and all navies — at once. Let us scrap the entire military and naval machine, down to the last button on the last drummer boy's tunic.' At which sweeping suggestion (I believe it was made in all good faith) the great powers threw up their hands in horror.

'Is he going to speak?'

'Yes. But ssh! The conference is beginning.'

I leant forward, thrilled.

But . . . what was happening?

Why were people still talking, laughing, moving about? The conference was beginning, certainly. A little man, whom I recognized as Politis, the Greek, was already pouring out polite phrases through the microphone. I heard the word *securité*, *securité*, *securité*, over and over again, and I remember thinking, rather vaguely, that it was queer for any real pacifist to mention the word *securité* so often without once mentioning the word 'peace'. But that was not what really worried me. Politis might be talking nonsense, but surely the delegates might at least pretend to listen?

They are not listening. They are not even looking in the speaker's direction. Their backs are turned to him — not in any gesture of protest, but in obvious boredom. Look at that delegate there, holding the *Journal de Genève* up before him, turning its pages flippantly, right under the nose of Politis himself. Doesn't he realize that there are millions of men and women all over the world who regard this conference as their one hope — who follow its proceedings with a dumb eagerness far greater than that which they would show in any Church service? Would this delegate continue to read his *Journal de Genève* in church?

There is another delegate just below, with his head on the table and his hands sprawled out in front of him. Is he asleep? And if so, in God's name why is he not woken up, and turned out into the street, and his place taken by any of the men and women whom he has the effrontery to 'represent' — the men and women who want to get something done?

The conference has been on for nearly half an hour, yet the delegates are still streaming in. Is there nobody in authority here, nobody to reprimand them? A schoolmaster does not allow little boys to come in late for their history lesson. Little boys have to learn history. And what about the little men who are *making* it? Can they stroll in when they like . . . picking their teeth, waving to friends in the gallery?

Securité — securité — securité!' The words ring out, time and again, in this dreadful speech. I turn to my friend to try to find some explanation of it all. He only shakes his head, and shrugs his shoulders. I feel betrayed, humiliated. Is there not a single honest man here? Is there not one man who will cease, even for a moment, from laughing and chattering and whispering?

I stare round me in desperation. My eyes light on a little cocotte in the gallery, a few yards away. She is a pretty little thing with sultry lips and purple eyelids set in a face as white as a Christmas rose. A group of delegates see her. They nudge each other. They wink. She winks back. The conference is forgotten. The dead are forgotten. The living do not care. All that those delegates can see is a white face and lips of a geranium-red, luring them from above.

VIII

The clock hand had twice made the full circle. The atmosphere was hellish. The delegates reclined in attitudes of awkward somnolence.

And then Litvinoff got up to speak.

It was my last hope. I was unutterably depressed. Dazed by the heat, distracted by the irreverent jabber around me, disgusted by everything and everybody, I watched Litvinoff edging his way to the tribune. He looked in earnest. I prayed that he was . . . that he would say something to wake these sluggards. People were sitting up, too, and putting down their papers, turning round their chairs and adjusting their glasses. That was a good sign. Perhaps at last the spell was going to be broken.

'*Meesterprep Zeedent!*'

His voice rang out in a husky wail. I turned to my friend, in an access of despair. 'He's speaking in Russian!'

'I'm not so sure. Listen!'

'*Asti farter rummeler.*'

'No, it's German, I think.'

'Or Italian?'

The husky wail continued. It was like no language I had ever heard before. Was it by any chance Esperanto? But no—one knew, from occasional experience, that Esperanto had, at least, certain familiar phrases. But this—this was like a compound of Scotch and Basque.

Wait a minute, though! He is warming up. It is a little clearer now. And surely that was a sentence one could recognize . . . something very like 'the French plan?' Here is another 'We have heard of security . . .' True, the pronunciation is unbelievably grotesque, like a reflection in a laughing mirror, but all the same. . . .

I turned to my friend:

'I *believe* he's speaking English.'

'I was going to say the same . . . but . . .'

'Listen.'

At exactly this moment a phrase in quite unmistakable English came from Litvinoff's lips. I do not know if it was particularly funny, but I began to laugh. And once I had begun, I could not stop. The heat, the disappointment, the boredom, the mockery, the *everything* . . . it was too much. I could not stop. I was hysterical.

I stuffed my handkerchief to my mouth, grabbed my hat, rose to my feet, said 'pardon' a great many times, trod heavily on the cocotte's toes, and scrambled through the exit door. There was an open window opposite me. I stood in front of it, breathing deep the clean air of the mountains. Then I walked down the stairs, through the swing doors, and across the road.

I looked out over the lake. The sun was just beginning to set.

IX

I stood there, shivering. I said to myself:

'You might as well go away, at once. You could catch the night train to Paris. You would get to the Gare de Lyon soon after ten, and you would drive out to the Bois to see if the hazels had begun to shoot. Shoot. Shoot! That's a funny word to use about a pretty little thing like a hazel . . .

'You could drive back and go and see if there was anybody in the Ritz bar. Probably Cole Porter would be there, drinking *citron pressé*. He would come up and ask if you could think of anything to rhyme with the duck-billed platypus, because he's writing a lot of lyrics for the new Cochran show. Jean might be there, and Pierre — but no, they're doing their military service. You could lunch somewhere alone, and go to see a news-reel film. But the film would be nothing but soldiers marching. . . .'

Life seemed to have lost all purpose. Is it odd for any man to become so morbidly dejected by disillusionment over an abstraction like the League of Nations? Ought a man to keep such despairing mood for the occasions when he is betrayed by his mistress? Perhaps. But, you see, for a very long period I had felt that civilization was drifting, ever more swiftly, to utter destruction, and that the only harbour in sight was Geneva. Now, Geneva seemed only a mirage after all. I was condemned to live and die in a mad and purposeless world.

The sun had almost sunk, and the mountains were

rimmed with gold. One would have thought that men who worked in the shadow of such mountains would absorb something of their tranquillity, but it seems that they only regarded them as a back-cloth for their own follies. To me they are many things, in many moods . . . white flowers and spirits and birds, and all things white, all things in the colour of God, which is an ecstasy of all colours. And sometimes I could see them not at all, but only the great hosts of outstretched arms behind them — the waving fields of pleading arms, uplifted to the City of Peace which they cannot see.

X

I stood against the bar, and laughed and laughed.

It was barely an hour later, but in that brief space my whole outlook had changed. No, I had not gone into the town to drown my sorrows. My laughter was due to no alcoholic intoxication, for I had consumed nothing more potent than orange juice. It was due to a fact so simple that it will probably bore you. Let me explain.

After the gloomy meditation by the side of the lake, I was just preparing to walk back to the hotel, and pack up for Paris, when I was hailed by a voice from the twilight. I looked round and saw a cheerful young man, who, for reasons which you will soon observe, must remain anonymous. We will call him X. He is a very brilliant journalist and is one of the best foreign correspondents in Geneva.

'God — if it isn't Beverley Nichols!'

'Hullo X,' I said, without any marked enthusiasm.

'What are you doing in this town?'

'I came to search for Peace.' I must have said it with a very stagey bitterness, because X only laughed.

'You look as if you'd caught something. What's up?'

I sighed. What was the use of explaining it all? X was notoriously a realist and a cynic. He didn't care tuppence to what chaos the world was drifting, as long as he had front seats to watch it all. On the other hand, I felt like talking to somebody. So I leant back against the wall, lit a cigarette, and told him exactly what I thought of Geneva, with particular reference to the farce which I had just seen enacted in the disarmament hall.

Before I had said half I wanted to say, X interrupted me.

'But Good Lord, man, you've got it all wrong.'

'In what way?'

'Well, you don't imagine that any business is done at these conferences?'

'I have been deploring that fact for the last five minutes.'

'Don't be dense, you fool. Don't you realize that those meetings are a mere formality, that all the business is done beforehand?'

'I don't understand.'

Then X leant forward and took me by the arm, and told me something which may sound very dull to you; but was tremendously significant to me, something which began the extraordinary change of mood, previously recorded. He said:

'*All the delegates have had printed copies of this afternoon's speeches for the last twenty-four hours. They've read them, digested them, discussed them. The attendance at this afternoon's meeting is really only a formality . . .'*

'What's that?' I still did not realize the full significance of what he was saying.

He repeated his information, a little impatiently. And then said '*Now* do you still feel so disgusted? Now don't you think that even you might get a bit bored listening to a speech you'd already *read*, perhaps six times? Don't you think even *you* might take out a newspaper and glance at it to relieve the monotony?'

He added. 'I don't object to your being an idealist. But really, my dear fellow, you ought to take the trouble to acquaint yourself with the facts. And now let's go back and see what's happening.'

I entered the building a good deal more happily than I emerged from it. I found it a little difficult to explain this sudden elation to X, who seemed to think me extremely stupid. He said:

'But wasn't it obvious, man? Even if they hadn't had printed copies of the speeches, what was the use of listening? Half the speeches are absolutely unintelligible because the pronunciation is so bad.'

Thinking of Litvinoff, I agreed fervently.

'Besides — think of having to listen to every speech twice, in French and English! I suppose you *did* realize that each speech was translated as soon as it had been delivered?'

'Dimly.'

'Well, wouldn't that excuse a good deal of walking about and inattention?'

'It would. But why do they want to meet at all? Why don't they settle everything in their hotels?'

'Because, my innocent lad, it ought to be evident to anybody of the meanest intelligence that if they merely did that, Geneva would just become a buzzing hive of intrigue, and the whole principle of the League would go to pot. It's all very well to make nice little plans and decisions over a dinner table, but if you have to get up on your hind legs on the following day, and tell the whole world what you've been talking about, you're inclined to watch your step. That's the difference between the old diplomacy and the new.'

'Then you really are pro-League of Nations?'

'Personally, of course. Nobody could live at Geneva for a year, as I've done, without being pro-League of Nations — personally.'

'What do you mean by "personally"?'

X abruptly changed the conversation.

XI

This time we did not go up to the Strangers' Gallery. We went into the Press Room.

The Press Room at the League of Nations is considerably more imposing, both in size and in content, than the rooms usually allotted to newspaper men. It is a very long hall, running the whole length of the building, and it is fitted with bars, and alcoves, and other devices for encouraging conversation. Moreover it is by no means a Press Room only. It is a favourite meeting place for all the chief delegates, and it is here over a cup of tea, or a glass of champagne, that a great many important decisions are taken.

The place is a bustle of activity. Journalists dart up and down, delegates stand in the centre of the hall, being interviewed (i.e. folding their arms, looking at their boots, and keeping their lips tightly sealed) — an occasional Prime Minister talks to an occasional foreign secretary. It is a vivid and impressive spectacle, and yet, it is quite without formality. The newest and least important journalist can go up and buttonhole Sir John Simon without any fear of a rebuff. Whether the journalist gains either instruction or pleasure from the contact is another question.

The hall is something new in history. The world has never seen anything even faintly resembling it before. There have been conferences, yes, and congresses, alliances, holy and unholy. From the dawn of history, the victors have met the vanquished. From the earliest, whispering records we hear the lisp of princes, intriguing in halls long crumbled, plotting, spying, dividing the spoils. The great ones have met together, a thousand times, on fields of gold and on fields of blood. But never before have they met like this, never before have they been brought together by a sense of the unity of mankind.

For that is what it is, even if it sounds pompous. For what other reason do Colombia, and China, and England, and Siam, and France and Jugo-Slavia and Rumania and Persia and Italy and all the rest of them — sixty four nations in all — meet together? Over and over again you read, in capitalist newspapers all over the world — that the League is not 'representative' because it does not contain America or Russia. That does not alter the fact that it is infinitely more 'representative' than any other group of nations which the world has ever known.

More of this later. It remains to point the moral and adorn the tale.

I sat in that hall with X, watching the world file by. We talked of the Japanese crisis, which is old history now. We talked of disarmament, which, at the moment of writing, is unrecorded history.

'Something really *is* being done,' said X.

'I wish I could think the same.'

'Well — at least we've reached this position — that the nation which increases its armaments has damned well got to explain itself to the rest of the world. Isn't that something?'

'Yes . . . but . . .'

'But what?'

'If only the *people* could be made to realize that. If only the press of the world wouldn't always sneer. Now, *you're* all right. I don't read your newspaper, but I imagine you'll cable back a pretty encouraging report?'

'Do you?'

There was a curious, furtive look in X's eyes.

'Well . . . after what you've been saying . . .'

X looked away from me. In a cold, dry voice he said, 'D'you know what the main title of my story will be to-night?'

'No.'

' "*Geneva asleep! The League Discredited*".'

'I don't understand.'

'Don't you? Very well . . . here's the beginning of the story.' He drew a crumpled wad of manuscript from his pocket and began to read. 'Another staggering blow was dealt to the moribund League of Nations this afternoon when' . . .

He crumpled up the manuscript and put it in his pocket. He rose to his feet. He grinned.

'You see,' he said, 'my paper doesn't like the League of Nations.'

'But you . . .'

'Oh! *Me!* I'm a newspaper man. And a damned good one, too.'

He was.

CHAPTER IX

THE LEAGUE AND THE LIARS

'Do you ever give up hope?'

'No!'

'Never?'

'N-n-no!'

After which we both paused and gasped.

Not a brilliant dialogue, you may agree, but the room in which it took place was so hot that it was miraculous that men could talk in it at all. The room belonged to Mr. Arthur Henderson, the president of the Disarmament Conference, with whom I had made an immediate appointment, after the grim little episode which closed the last chapter.

By now I had become fairly hardened to the heat of the hotels in Geneva. I was able to sit, for considerable periods, in rooms like Turkish baths, with nothing more than a slight headache and a feeling of faint nausea. But Mr. Henderson received me in a furnace. There is no other word for it. I swear that the very wood of the chair he offered me was hot, merely through the temperature of the room. In addition, I had to sit opposite him, with a particularly brilliant sun blazing in my eyes, so that I only saw a black patch where his face was. Such conditions are not conducive to clear thinking nor to brilliant conversation, so the reader must make allowances.

Henderson struck me as a man who was desperately sincere but desperately tired. He did not move once from the posture he adopted when I entered the room. There was a heavy droop to his eyelids and his voice lagged. And yet, he was unbeaten. He said:

'If you could see some of the telegrams I am receiving every hour of the day you would not ask me if I ever gave up hope. They are amazing. Only this morning there has been a sheaf of telegrams from organizations of young Americans, urging me on, wishing me good luck.' Then he added, 'I think I shall take some of them in to the Conference this afternoon to read when I am listening to——!' (And here he mentioned the name of a particularly irritating delegate whose speeches were as vague as the folds of drapery round an allegorical figure of Patriotism.)

'But you surely aren't satisfied with what has been done?'

'Satisfied?' He laughed, rather sadly. 'No I'm not satisfied!' And then, it was as though he were speaking to himself. 'We have been at this job for a year,' he said, 'and nation after nation still gets up and talks about "Justice", and "Security", and "Liberty" and "The Necessities of the Situation". They invent elaborate metaphors. They make endless perorations. It is really almost heartbreaking to have to listen to it, day in and day out, because the will to peace *is* there . . . don't make any mistake about that . . . but it is being lost in a cloud of words.'

'Let me give you an example. You may have noticed, in the speeches you've been hearing in the last few days, that if a delegate says the word "disarmament" once in five minutes, he says the word "security" at least three times. That, of course, is merely an example of the Fear which has all the nations still in its grip — the Fear that we are doing our utmost to eradicate. Well, after endless discussions I have at last persuaded them to attack these two problems separately, to work along two lines, to work out the minimum of "security" and also to work out the minimum of "disarmament" and to see if we cannot make these two lines meet.'

'And you think they will meet?'

'Yes — I think so. In the end.'

He went on to discuss matters which it would be a betrayal of confidence to report. But I cannot refrain from quoting the last words he said to me, as I was going:

'Remember this, young man — *the League is what we choose to make it*. If you are dissatisfied with the League's progress, don't blame the League. Blame the governments behind it. And blame the Press that moulds the opinion of those governments. And blame the secret influences that mould the opinion of the Press!'

II

Always it was the same tale. The enemies of the League were not inside it, but outside it.

I went to another session of the disarmament conference. I was lucky enough to choose an occasion when, for once in a way, a speech was being made which had not been previously circulated among the delegates. And this time there was no inattention, no whispering, and no late comers. The change was amazing. One felt that here the pacific intelligence of the world was concentrated — that great movements were afoot.

I went to cafés where groups of delegates, representing as much power as their governments would allow them, sat over their coffee talking till the small hours. I heard scraps of conversation which made me want to join in — discussions of plans, figures, statistics, quite open references to matters which were supposed to be secret.

That is one remarkable and very happy characteristic of the Geneva 'atmosphere' . . . the delegates have no secrets from one another. The press gives you the idea that they are all intriguing violently, that the air is thick with the mutter of plot and counterplot. That is a lie. The 'secrets' exist in the mind of the press only. In Geneva everything is open.

You really must get a clear realization of the way in which the public opinion of the world, as formed by the great popular newspapers, is being misled on this vital issue. I am a journalist myself, dependent for a large proportion of my income on the whims of newspaper proprietors (who on the whole are honest, decent men, tragically misguided), so I trust that you will at least grant that I am disinterested in my criticism of them. It is my firm conviction that the great newspaper proprietors of the world could stop the possibility of war in a few months, if they could ever be persuaded to see the light.

As an example of the irresponsibility of the press I might quote a conversation I had with Count Bernstorff, whom I met the day after my interview with Henderson. Bernstorff, to the English speaking world, is best known for the role he played as German ambassador in America during the war.

He sat opposite me at a party, consuming innumerable cups of weak tea, and occasionally stretching out a very white and delicate hand, exquisitely framed in a long glistening cuff, over a tray of marrons glacés. And he said exactly what Henderson had said:

'*The League is what we choose to make it!*'

His diagnosis of the situation was so similar to Henderson's that it need not be quoted. And he too had some acid things to say about the press. Remembering my schoolboy impressions of Bernstorff as a sort of arch-demon, hovering like a black bat over the white body of America during the war, I asked him to elaborate the picture.

'The press accused me of every crime under the sun,' he said.

'Murder?'

'As a matter of course. And arson. And robbery. And . . . and how do you say it . . . r-r-r-rape?'

'Not quite how I say it, but very nicely said.'

'And of course,' he added, 'I was constantly accused of making a fortune out of the war. When Wilson sent his first peace note, there was a great slump on Wall Street. All the heavy industries had been growing rich by exporting war material, and they were afraid that their time of harvest was over. Well, on the day after Wilson sent his note, the newspapers came out with scare headlines about me. How I had been the only person who knew that Wilson was going to send the note. How I had sold stocks "short". How I had been making my "guilty millions". As a matter of fact, I made it a strict rule never to touch American stocks during the war, for obvious reasons. I'm very glad I didn't.'

'Well — I had to see the reporters. I could not let those charges go unanswered. But I did not tell them a long story. I simply stood up to them, and looked them straight in the eyes, and I said "Do you believe it?"'

'One reporter had the courage to say "No."'

'I sighed with relief. And I said "Well, I don't believe it either."'

'And the extraordinary thing about it was that my very simple remark seemed to tickle the American sense of humour. "I don't believe it either". That was quoted all over the United States, and they thought it a huge joke.'

'Ever since then,' added Bernstorff, 'I have had a very high opinion of the American sense of humour.'

To compensate for this irrelevancy, I would like to quote a judgment of Bernstorff, concerning the League of Nations, which struck me as highly significant. We were discussing the possibility of Japan leaving the League. Everybody was saying, in Geneva, that if Japan left, it would be a 'death-blow' to the League. Bernstorff denied that strenuously. He gave a great many reasons, too long and elaborate to quote, but the main tenor of his argument was that the League was such a vital necessity, and that men *knew* it to be such a vital necessity, that it would survive, and gradually grow stronger.

I said to him 'If men *know* that it is the only light left in an utterly dark world, why do they all try to blow it out?'

To which he answered 'That is only one of the many paradoxes of human nature to which I am still seeking an answer.'

III

Thus the days went by, while I wandered about at will, gathering impressions. And the more I saw of the League and its work, the more I felt that here at last was a real internationalism, a real sense that the world, at last, had found some central directing force, if only the world would listen.

I spent hours in the library, with its amazingly polyglot collection of works of reference. (It would need a page to give a list of the number of *Who's Who*, in various languages.) I went to lunch with Benes, the minister for Czecho-Slovakia, and drank delicious Swiss wine while he gave a brilliant exposition of the political situation of Central Europe. I explored the old Geneva, which nobody knows, and descended into cafés in dungeons, where one ate *fondu* — a luscious confection made with cheese and milk and wine. The dish is placed in the centre of the table and everybody shares it, dipping into it with his bread, and dragging the bread out, covered with hot creamy stuff that begins to solidify just as you are popping it into your mouth.

I saw everybody who mattered and a great many who didn't. As each day passed the League seemed more and more obviously essential. Geneva seemed sane and the rest of the world took on deepening hues of insanity.

Mind you, it would be much easier for me, and probably a good deal more profitable, from every conceivable point of view, to write cheap satire about the League. There is always a market for *that!* And, needless to say, the material is ready to hand. For example, there is endless comic material in the new League of Nations building, which is springing up on the shores of the Lake. 'Springing up' is a good expression in some ways, and bad in others. For though it looks as though it were going to jump at you, its construction has been a depressingly tardy business.

It looks like the Vatican of a Mechanistic Pope. Thousands of blank windows stare into the wintry sunlight. Miles of shiny drains expose themselves above the bleak turf. Acres of white paint glitter over singularly square surfaces.

Was this the Palace of Peace? I sighed as I asked myself this question. They had told me that five — or was it seven? — architects combined their energies to produce it. That fifty — or was it seventy? — nations had to sit in judgment on the final designs. That the Colombian minister had to poke his nose into the smallest clothes cupboard, and that the delegate for Guatemala worked himself into a frenzy over the precise shade of green which went to tint the garage doors. That every little bustling nobody swarmed in and out of the building saying 'do this', 'do that' and 'do the other', until the building ceased to be a Palace of Peace and became, instead, a Tower of Babel.

Was this the system to which I was pledged to give my heart and soul? Thus, sadly, did I question myself as I prowled round those barrack erections. If this was the result of internationalism in art, what would be its result in *real-politik* Would we be faced with a world as bleak and formless as this building? And if so, would it not be better to give up the whole thing, to let the strong be strong and the weak be weak? To let the conquerors conquer, and seize the fair open spaces of the world, and build upon them palaces of arrogance and beauty?

IV

Such depressing moments, however, were short lived. The conviction remained that the League was a great and shining tribute to man's essential unity, in whatever building it might be housed.

Now, it is almost impossible to hope that you will not be bored if I venture to suggest, even with extreme diffidence, that this is the moment for me to make a little speech which will sum up the convictions I gained from my stay in Geneva. 'Why the League of Nations is Necessary' by Beverley Nichols, is the sort of thing which one simply does not read. I am bitterly aware of that. However it is the sort of thing which one is impelled to write, and so you can skip the next few pages if you like. Yet, I hope you won't. Because they may irritate you.

Here, then, is the little article.

'Why The League of Nations is Necessary.'

It will be simplest if our arguments are addressed to an

imaginary *opponent* of the League of Nations. And the word with which we shall endeavour to convince him is the word 'anarchy'.

This is what we shall say to him:

'Anarchy! You dislike the word? It has an evil tang? The theory of *anarchy*, as you understand it, appals you?

'Then why do you support it? Why do you sing hymns in praise of it? Why do you sneer at honest men who think that *anarchy* is not the best system?

'You say you don't do these things? Then may I ask you what is the system that governs the European powers, if you deny the validity or the value or, indeed, the necessity, of the League of Nations? What *is* the name of this system? If any country can do what it likes, if, for example, France can declare war on Italy without consulting any other authority, what is the name for the European system then? Is it anything else than anarchy? I really want you to answer this question.

'To help you to formulate your answer, may I, in all humility, suggest that you "personify" your nations? Nations are very like individuals. And therefore it will be simpler if you think of England as a nice stolid old man, France as a robust female, Germany as a pipe-smoking Fritz, Holland as a girl with wooden shoes, Italy as a fiery troubadour, Russia as a moujik, etc. etc. You may tell me that it is all very childish, but it is not really so very far from the truth.

'You have thought of these odd people? You have a clear mental picture of them? Well — imagine that they all came to live in a little village that you know of. And then, imagine if you can, that the local authorities, in a fit of midsummer madness, suddenly said, "As far as these people are concerned, we will suspend all laws, withdraw the police and allow them to do exactly as they think fit. If they quarrel, they must fight it out with their fists, or with whatever implements they may find handy."

'What happens? Anarchy — in the first week. The Italian drives on the wrong side of the road, because he is used to doing that, and collides with John Bull. Madame France empties her slops into Schmidt's garden, who in turn makes night impossible for all the inhabitants by playing a super-gramophone till the small hours. The Russian moujik robs all the hen roosts. John Bull tries to stop anybody else bathing in the village pond. A group of noisy neighbours, called the Balkans, set fire to the village pub., etc. etc. etc.

'Would you like to live in such a village? You *are* living in it — or in a very good equivalent of it. And yet you throw up your hands in horror when we suggest that really, a policeman might make life a little more enjoyable, even if he did require you to obey certain regulations.'

V

Nobody knows, more clearly than I know myself, that the foregoing arguments are childish. They are the sort of arguments that ought to be written on a black-board by an elementary schoolmistress, while hot little boys make rude faces behind her back, and wonder when she is going to begin to draw animals. Nevertheless though they are childish, they are true — as true as any chalked and elementary symbols about 2 and 2 making 4.

And the reason they are childish is because Europe is childish. I beg your pardon. I am flattering Europe. Intelligent children usually elect, or acknowledge, some leader. Intelligent children, when they are playing games, abrogate a certain amount of their sovereignty. They realize that games are not really very much fun if everybody makes his own rules.

We have not yet reached the intellectual heights of intelligent children. We still insist upon making our own rules. The dirtiest peasant in the most barren country still salutes his brave little flag with precisely the same emotions as the most august big-wig in England salutes the Union Jack.

It would be wicked and 'unmanly' if he didn't. Wouldn't it?

For the answer, see the next chapter.

CHAPTER X

LORD BEAVERBROOK IS TOO BUSY

I ADMIRE Lord Beaverbrook, because I think that any man who can make one half of the world wonder if he is a saint, and the other half of the world quite certain that he is a devil (while he himself keeps an open mind on the subject), has guts.

A bad man, Lord Beaverbrook, but a vivid one. That is my opinion. And yet, am I justified in using the adjective 'bad'? Is any man who stands in front of a mirror, making speeches at it, and seeing things which are not there . . . is he actually a bad man? Or is he just a man with straws in his hair?

I only once met Lord Beaverbrook. He was extremely courteous to me, and he has a charm you could cut with a knife. I have often heard him speak. He is a grand speaker. An ugly little dynamo, with staccato gestures. And like all great speakers, opposition is fuel to him. He eats up hecklers. He catches a hostile sentence from the air, grabs at it, twists it into a completely different shape, and flings it back in the face of his opponent before the wretched man has time to get his breath.

Bad? Good? What are those words? Somehow, Beaverbrook evades them. Because, in spite of the violence of my opposition to him, in spite of the fact that sometimes I feel that the *Daily Express* is a newspaper unworthy of the most degrading service to which the human body could put it, I cannot make up my mind that the man is a hypocrite. Which makes the tragedy all the more damnable.

II

Hypocrisy!

That is the note on which the first phrase of this little duel opens.

You see, it was inevitable, after setting down the somewhat childish arguments in the last chapter, that I should try to deepen those arguments and extend them, and clothe them in respectable language. I also wanted to test them in the fires of opposition.

Obviously I had not the political knowledge nor experience necessary to advance many steps beyond the position I had reached. If I had been decently educated, I might have managed it. But I had received only the normal education of the young English gentleman, and after that, I had to work out my own salvation.

This was a matter in which it was necessary to call in outside help. I wanted a man of international reputation and international outlook who would put the case for the League of Nations, as I could not put it. I also wanted a man of international reputation and *national* outlook to try to combat his arguments.

So I pitted Sir Norman Angell against Lord Beaverbrook. Angell is not only a fine pacifist but has a great legal mind. He has a brain as clear as crystal. If he could be made educational dictator of the world, war would vanish like the morning mist, in a single generation. He foretold the future, in his book *The Great Illusion*, far more clearly than any man of his generation.

I wrote to Angell and asked him to meet Lord Beaverbrook. He said he would be delighted to do so, at any time and at any place. I then wrote to Lord Beaverbrook and asked him to meet Sir Norman Angell. He replied that he would be glad to answer any questions Angell might put to him, *by post*.

'*If you get Angell to ask me questions*,' he wrote, '*I will answer them*.'

It was then that he struck the first blow to which I referred when I opened this section with the word 'hypocrisy'.

'I read a book of Angell's not long ago,' wrote Lord Beaverbrook. 'He says I am a hypocrite. Therefore I say he is a fool. For why? Because, of my many vices, hypocrisy is not in the list. Anybody but a fool would be aware of that fact.'

This little outburst warmed my heart. If A (who thinks that B is a hypocrite), meets B (who thinks that A is a fool), the result is likely to be enlivening, even if it is not instructive.

I had several conversations with Angell before he wrote the letter which appears below. We came to the conclusion that it would be best to pin Lord Beaverbrook down to his 'isolationist' policy . . . i.e. the policy which advocates a self-supporting and politically exclusive British Empire as an alternative to the League of Nations.

I had two reasons for narrowing the issue. Firstly, because Beaverbrook, through his press, has persuaded quite a formidable body of electoral opinion that the isolationist policy is possible, and morally and economically defensible. Secondly, because if the isolationist policy is defeated and exposed, the League of Nations immediately presents itself to the intelligent reader as the only possible alternative.

It was a dull rainy morning when I received Angell's letter, and I opened it in fear and trembling. I was terribly afraid that he might have failed me — that the letter would be boring, or unconvincing, or that it would miss out important points. But when I had read it, I breathed a sigh of relief.

This was unanswerable! The 'fool' had produced a masterpiece. Like a great criminal lawyer, he had put Lord Beaverbrook in the dock, and 'submitted him to a remorseless fire of cross-examination'. I felt, after reading that letter, that I could defy any man to answer it, without 'hypocrisy', and remain an 'honest imperialist'.

You will be impatient to read the letter. Here it is. Please read it slowly.

III

4 King's Bench Walk,
Temple,
London, E.C.4.

My Dear Beverley Nichols,

I am sorry Lord Beaverbrook won't have a talk, but am glad he will answer questions. I should have liked a talk because there are a good many of us who do sincerely want to understand the reasons which prompt him to oppose any attempt to change the old international anarchy; which lead him to suppose that, if maintained, it can have any result other than the one it always has had; results which become cumulatively more disastrous.

It is a question first and last of Britain's defence — defence of her political independence, of her prosperity, freedom from unemployment, the industry and trade by which she lives, of the financial apparatus indispensable to it, of the stability of the money in which it is done. I would therefore put these questions.

(1) Does Lord Beaverbrook agree that those things are most endangered by war, whether it be victorious or not, since victory has not enabled us to defend our trade, which dwindles and dwindles; nor our investments; nor our monetary system; nor prevent disastrous financial collapse, nor the disruption of our empire? (The economic nationalism within the Empire, expressed by much higher tariff barriers and entirely new ones as in India and Ireland, is due largely to the dislocations created by the war.)

(2) Does he agree that if we pile on our already shaken and disordered economic system the further dislocations, unpayable debts, revolutions, which we now know are the necessary legacy of war and which so shook the relatively sound system of 1914, then it will probably finish off the present order in chaos?

(3) Is it Lord Beaverbrook's general view that the best way to prevent that recurrence is to continue the old armament competition and decline to discuss international

agreement or organization? If so, on what ground does he believe that the old method will not produce the old result?

(4) For a nation to be secure under the competitive principle it must be stronger than any probable rival. What becomes of the rival? Is he to go without defence? How shall defence of each be managed under this plan, since the security of one means the insecurity of the other? Does Lord Beaverbrook think there is some system by which each can be stronger than the other?

(5) If, in order to be secure, we make ourselves stronger than a rival, does Lord Beaverbrook suggest that that rival will accept the situation and not resort to alliance making? And if that rival makes alliances are we to refrain from resorting to the same weapon? And alliance is an arm, like a battleship, or a submarine, adding to a nation's power. Are we to leave this arm entirely in the hands of prospective rivals?

(6) From the time of Julius Cæsar to Kaiser Wilhelm there has not been a single century in which we have not been drawn into the affairs of the Continent. Does Lord Beaverbrook really believe that, if isolationism was not possible even for a remote island in ancient times, a great Empire in the days of the aeroplane can continue to pursue isolationism?

(7) To keep ourselves free of general or permanent commitments and be guided by each circumstance as it arises, was the method we pursued before the war. Although we had no League Commitments in 1914 and ministers were up to the last proclaiming how free our hands were, we were drawn in. Does Lord Beaverbrook

think we could have kept out, that our entrance was a mistake?

(8) If he thinks our entrance a mistake, would he have regarded the victory of the Germanic powers, the creation, that is, of an hegemony so preponderant that we could not have resisted any demands it cared to make upon us, as a matter of indifference? If so why trouble about armaments at all — if it is a matter of indifference that combinations much stronger than we are, should arise?

(9) If, on grounds of national security, we cannot accept the preponderance of a foreign combination, why should we expect foreigners to accept ours, especially as our preponderance resulted in imposing upon our rival a Treaty which Lord Beaverbrook himself now declares to be outrageously unjust?

(10) When that Treaty was under discussion did Lord Beaverbrook's press support the efforts of those who desired to moderate its terms? Or did it attack those 'pro-Germans' with bitter personal abuse and raise against them easily excited nationalist prejudices?

(11) On the eve of the war Sir Edward Grey declared that the only possible alternative to the see-saw of the Balance of Power, by which the precarious defence of one was achieved by depriving the other of all defence, was for both to pool their power to secure the observance of a common rule of international life like arbitration of disputes: to build up what Asquith called the community of Power behind the law. That this indeed is the alternative is the declared view of every British Prime Minister, every Foreign Minister since the war, of practically every competent student of political science. On

what general grounds does Lord Beaverbrook differ from practically all the British statesmen and all the competent students in view of the fact that he says (*Sunday Express*, September 11th): 'I am no authority on European politics. I cannot speak their language. I don't want to. I don't know their politicians. I don't like them?'

(12) It is common ground — presumably — that the prevention of a repetition of 1914 and its economic and financial consequences is both vital and difficult; that ultimately a more international habit of thought will be necessary; that it is worth some effort.

Lord Beaverbrook has declared persistently and violently that the League is too costly an effort; has created the impression that it is a grave burden on our national finances. Its cost bears the same relation to our national income that an annual contribution of half-a-crown does to a man with an income of about £3,000 a year. We have just added to estimates a sum more than twenty times our contribution to the League without one word from his press about the burden of this addition to our taxation. Does Lord Beaverbrook regard the harping upon the cost of the League as a fair presentation of the facts to the British public?

Yours very sincerely,
(Signed) Norman Angell.

P.S. Lord Beaverbrook believes in large economic units, the Empire rather than the British Isles, the larger the better. If, therefore, Denmark or Argentina applied for admission to the *Economic* Empire, said 'we will grant Britain every concession which the most Liberal of the

Dominions grant in return for the same concessions' would Lord Beaverbrook favour acceptance of the offer? If a preferential arrangement between Canada and Britain is good for Britain why should an exactly similar arrangement between Argentine and Britain be bad?

IV

I feel that even if there were no other reason for publishing this book, Sir Norman Angell's letter would have given me one.

I had copies made of it. I hovered impatiently over my secretary while she finished them. I ran out to the letter box at the end of the street, and posted it. And then I sat down and waited for a reply.

I waited more and more impatiently. I felt that sparks must be flying in the *Daily Express* office. I visualized Beaverbrook straining every nerve, calling upon all his expert knowledge and his intellectual resources. For after all, one does not allow a 'fool' to run one through, to riddle one, without a fight — not if one is an Empire Crusader.

And then the postman knocked. This was what fell on the floor:

Stornoway House,
Cleveland Row,
St. James's.
6th April, 1933.

Dear Mr. Nichols,

Thank you for your letter, and the enclosures from Sir Norman Angell.

When I said I would answer his questions, I had no idea that I should be confronted with such an immense catechism.

It would take me a great deal of labour and time to answer the questions as they should be answered. In the busy life I lead, I do not have the opportunity to do so. It is too big a proposition for me.

I must ask you to forgive me if I cannot carry out the task. I am so sorry that you and Sir Norman Angell have been put to any trouble. Will you please convey my apologies to him?

Yours sincerely,
Beaverbrook.

Well . . . there we are.

I quite agree that it would take any man 'a great deal of labour and time' to answer the questions as they should be answered. It would take him so much labour that by the time he had evolved the answers the British Empire might well have gone the way of all Empires, and the printing presses of the *Daily Express* might long have crumbled into dust.

However, on the chance that Lord Beaverbrook, who acts more quickly than the average man, may have a free week-end in the course of the next twelve months, I am publishing these questions, for all the world to see.

The 'fool' asked them. Will the 'hypocrite' reply?

CHAPTER XI

A CHRISTIAN COMES TO DINNER

It is here that we call for help.

I am getting muddled, and so, presumably, are you. I want a re-statement of belief, a re-orientation of doctrine. I began this book by swearing that I wouldn't fight in any circumstances. That oath was broken. I now seem to have committed myself to serving in an international army — to putting on a pair of white pants and ascending into the skies of Guatemala in order to gas negroes in the interests of Bolivia. It is a dreary prospect, and shows the extent to which a man's brain becomes addled if he tries to live like a gentleman and a Christian in twentieth century Europe.

A gentleman and a Christian! That phrase, no sooner written, suggested two men who might help me. Two men of very opposite points of view . . . Yeats Brown, the Bengal Lancer, who is certainly a gentleman, and Robert Mennel, ex-conscientious objector, who is certainly a Christian. (I am not suggesting that Mennel is not also a very charming 'gentleman', in the social sense, nor that Yeats Brown is not a Christian — though I believe that actually his religion is more near to the teachings of Buddha than of Christ. The only relevant fact is that I urgently needed help, and Yeats Brown and Mennel seemed the best men to argue the case out before me in its most extreme points of view.)

So I asked them both to dinner. They both said they would be delighted to come. But on the day of the dinner Yeats Brown had a swollen face, and could not dine. He rang up to ask us if we would go round and drink coffee with him after dinner, which we did. I was very sorry about Yeats Brown's face, because such nice faces ought not to be swollen, but in a way I was glad, because it gave me a chance to study, unhindered, the first conscientious objector I had ever met.

II

I must admit that when I was awaiting Mennel, before dinner, I was extremely nervous. I was afraid that he might be wildly impossible. A fanatic, a lunatic even — or worse, a nasty little skulking man with furtive eyes. I was quite prepared to hate him. To be made to feel unclean by him, to have my own faith shaken.

That shows you what early training does for a man. These fears which obsessed me were part of the inheritance of my school-days, when my elders and my betters used the phrase 'conscientious objector' as though it were something obscene. Over and over again I had been taught as a boy that these men were outcasts, social lepers. They were hardly to be spoken of in decent society. And though reason, in after years, had shown me the folly and injustice of this taboo, the original picture remained. And I stood in my study, waiting for the door to open, prepared to receive some figure that I felt would be repulsive to me.

Then he arrived. And these childish illusions were dispelled. For I met an extremely ordinary, kind-faced man of about fifty, with grey hair and amazingly candid eyes. He wore a black suit with grey striped trousers. He had beautiful hands and a pleasantly modulated voice. I heaved a sigh of relief. The bogy of my childhood vanished for ever. And we went down to dinner.

III

Now, if I had my way, I should cut dinner very short and go straight on to the dialogue between Mennel and Yeats Brown which you will find in the next chapter. But it is of little use for you to read a dialogue, however brilliant, if you have an unshaken prejudice against one of the speakers. And it is highly probable that you will have such a prejudice. Only yesterday I argued with a fairly representative young man whose mental attitude towards conscientious objectors was expressed by his final remark, which was 'Anyway, they're all dirty skunks and ought to have been strangled at birth.'

Mennel was so far from being a skunk, during the war, that although he was offered 'work of national importance', time and again, he refused it and preferred solitary confinement to a cushy job. He was put to every conceivable indignity. He was marched handcuffed through the main streets of his native town. He was mocked, sneered at, tried in a hundred fires. He was deserted by his friends, subjected to the mass contempt of a nation whose agony he shared and understood, although he was generally accused of being outside all that agony.

I believe in him absolutely. I believe that he is one of the most supremely honest men I have ever met. I believe that he is as near to a saint as any man I am ever likely to meet. I wish I could reproduce all his conversation at dinner. I can only give scraps. Here is one of them:

'It was right at the beginning,' he said, 'that I learnt that the only people from whom I was to expect sympathy were the soldiers, and not the civilians. When I was waiting in that first guard room, sitting down rather dazed on the floor, five men were bustled into the room, and the door was slammed on them. I made myself as inconspicuous as possible, hoping that they would not notice me. They were all in a towering rage. Their language was incredible. I gathered that they were all soldiers who, for some reason or other, either for breach of discipline or overstaying leave, were under arrest. They cursed and stormed for some time. Finally, they noticed me in my corner. They stopped swearing for a moment, and one of them walked up to me.

"What are you in here for, mate?"

'I thought it best to be as simple as possible, so I said:

'"Well, you see, I am a Quaker, and I refused to join the army, because I think that war is murder."

'The man took a step backwards. A terrible light came into his eyes. He raised his arm, which had a wound stripe on it. I thought that he was going to spring at me. The room was very silent.'

"Murder?" he whispered, "murder? It's *bloody* murder!"'

'And then we were friends. We had only a little while together, because the men were soon marched away, and I never saw them again. But as they went, they each came up to me, and shook me by the hand. "Stick to it, matey! Stick!" they said, one after another.'

IV

The point of view of the conscientious objector is so alien to the average man, who has been brought up with a Union Jack wrapped round him in his cot, who has learnt, in his history books, that his country has always been a divine favourite, and who, as a result, would think it dreadful if, after seeing an unpleasant French farce, he did not leap to his feet while an underpaid orchestra played 'God Save the King,' that it may be difficult for him to understand the spirit which prompted Mennel to prefer a dark and solitary cell to agreeable agricultural work in the open air. Granted that the average soldier, after a year's active service on the Western Front, would have regarded solitary confinement without much horror. (One could hardly suggest *any* ordeal which could compare in horror with his daily routine.) Still, solitary confinement can be, to say the least of it, irksome, especially when the door is held open for you to escape, if you will only betray your God.

'Over and over again,' said Mennel 'they offered me "work of National Importance" but I refused it. I could have left prison overnight, and been given some quite congenial occupation, if I had been prepared to put on uniform. I would not put it on. The officers could not understand it. "This is the softest job in the country we are offering," they said. I told them that I did not care.

'They were always trying to catch me out in their questions. At one court martial it was mentioned that one of the young Cadburys, who was a Quaker, had gone mine-sweeping. Why couldn't I go mine-sweeping too? they asked me. What objection could I have to that, in view of the fact that I should not be destroying life, but saving it? And I replied that I should be glad to go mine-sweeping, provided that they would give me permission to pick up all the mines in the world – British or German. They seemed to think that that reply was rather clever. It wasn't meant to be clever. It was merely honest, and was the only thing that a consistent man could say.'

If you are honest, you arrive at some queer conclusions. You have to say to the colonel in charge of your tribunal, as Mennel said, '*you* are organizing the country for victory and I am *not*', and you have to be able to show, consistently, why you aren't. You have to be able to answer such questions as 'Supposing you were ordered to make a khaki cap, what would you do?' You have to meet the twisters and the bluffers and the bullies, and you have to meet them alone. And sometimes, tired out, tortured, baffled, almost defeated, you have to say, wearily, 'I can't argue any more . . . I can only tell you what I feel.'

There was a man who said that or words very like it, on a similar issue, in the House of Commons during the war. 'I feel it, but I can't find the reason', he said. That man was Ramsay MacDonald, head of the 'National' Government.

O tempora, O mores!

V

Before we went on to drink coffee with Yeats Brown I asked Mennel a question which I had previously regarded as too delicate to put into words. I did not know how he would take it. But it had to be asked. You can probably realize what it was. I said:

'How many conscientious objectors were fakes?'

'Fakes?'

'Well — cowards?'

'Oh, I see.'

He smiled at me, so openly and spontaneously that I knew the question had not offended him. He considered for a moment. Then he said, 'I should think under two per cent.'

'What is your reason for saying that?'

'The cowards couldn't stand prison.'

'But if it was physical fear, and they had to choose between prison and the Front, wouldn't they choose prison?'

'No, that isn't the point. What I mean is, the *prison finds them out!* Only a man who was absolutely unshakable, who was true to the core, and who was prepared, if necessary, to sacrifice his life, could stand it. It was not a question so much of physical hardship, because every decent C.O. realized that what he was suffering was in no sort of way comparable with the infinitely greater horrors which were being suffered at the Front. No. It was more a spiritual question. Month after month of solitary confinement. Court-martial after court-martial. Cross-examination after cross-examination. The feeling that the entire world was against you. The endless *variety* of the arguments you had to meet. The abusive arguments. The threatening arguments. Worst of all, the arguments of men who really believed that you were sincere, but that you were misguided, and who were trying to save you from yourself. I am completely and finally convinced that only a man who was animated by a great faith could stand up to all that.'

And so am I.

Now, perhaps, I may hope that you will read the following chapter without fear, without favour, and, for a brief moment, without any memory of the patriotic cant which echoes all around us.

CHAPTER XII

'SKUNK' *VERSUS* BENGAL LANCER

The scene is YEATS BROWN's *little house in Knightsbridge. A pleasant yellow room with early hyacinths pushing their determined spears of perfume into the over-heated air.* YEATS BROWN's *face is not nearly so swollen as I feared, but I am gratified to see that it is slightly swollen, as I was afraid that he might have been merely excusing himself from dinner because he did not want to drink wine with* MENNEL *— or, even worse, because he mistrusted my cook.*

We sit by the fire, and almost instantly the two men engage with each other like well-trained wrestlers. I sit slightly in the background taking notes in a shorthand which is my own invention.

These notes formed the basis for this dialogue. Both YEATS BROWN *and* MENNEL *have revised them, corrected them, and made very extensive additions. As they stand, they echo, as truly as is ever likely to be echoed, the clash of temperament between the intelligent man of war and the intelligent man of peace.*

[*I will not further delay the reader.*]

Y. B. The first question I want to put to you is rather fundamental. Why do you regard peace as the highest issue in human life?

M. I don't. What I do say is that for settling

disputes or international problems the method of war is inexcusable.

Y. B. But most pacifists give the impression that they care more for peace than for their country's territory, liberty or honour.

M. That's unfortunate. It isn't true of us. We are devoted to our country and quick to defend her honour. What is true is that we entirely distrust military methods, particularly for the defence of spiritual things such as justice and liberty.

Y. B. But since you won't fight, how would you proceed to right the wrongs? Disarm, remain passive and fondly hope that things would right themselves?

M. Hardly. Pacifism is not passivism. Gandhi is the greatest living exponent of the pacifism that I believe in. There is no sentimental ignoring of vital wrong about him. The force he uses is the force of plain truth and love, but it is an active force. Towards his opponents he is not aggressive physically but his mind and emotions are exceedingly active, thinking constantly of all the possible ways of winning the truth for both sides. Gandhi is truly a Mahatma in this — a great soul.

Y. B. I quite agree that a thousand years hence Gandhi may be considered to have put his finger on some of the weak points of our civilization, particularly industrial civilization, but as to his not ignoring vital wrongs, he is doing that all the time. He preaches non-violence but the result is often bloodshed and rioting. He admitted for instance, that he was indirectly responsible for the unspeakable horrors of the Chari Chaura outrage. That's what your pacifism leads to, practically.

M. But has this got to go on for a thousand years? Gandhi's emphasis is for ever laid on the fact that his God is Truth as well as Love, and Truth for him implies just and true human relationships, such as are not possible either in industrial or any other kind of warfare.

Y. B. But don't truth and love apparently conflict sometimes?

M. How do you mean?

Y. B. Well, for example, when Christ drove the money-changers out of the temple. Do you mean that he was wrong to have done that?

M. I shouldn't have done it.

Y. B. No, you wouldn't have done it, but Christ did!

M. I have my doubts.

Y. B. What's that?

M. Quite frankly I question the details of the story. After all narratives are not always strictly correct. You have to use your own spiritual understanding. I can't see Jesus laying about him with a whip, nor Gandhi either for that matter.

Y. B. Yet Christ himself said, 'I come to bring not peace but a sword.'

M. And metaphorically speaking he did. Every new teacher challenging the existing order of things causes division and strife even amongst members of the same family. The sword in this phrase was surely a figure of speech. A physical, steel sword in the hands of Jesus is to me unthinkable.

Y. B. Not to me.

M. Do you mean to say that you can visualize Jesus with a sword or a bayonet in his hands?

Y. B. I can see him with a whip in his hands in the temple which is much the same thing. Christ knew that force was sometimes necessary in human affairs.

M. What about the incident of Peter drawing his sword in defence of his Master?

Y. B. Well, what about the incident of the young centurion? Jesus delighted in the young centurion and he never told him to resign from the army.

M. I admit that he never actually rebuked any soldiers as such.

Y. B. Then why should you assume that Christ is on your side?

M. I suppose the thing is instinctive. Jesus showed us a way of dealing with opponents or evilly disposed men that is entirely different from the military way.

II

Y. B. Do you visualize a world without pain?

M. Certainly not. Pain is a very necessary corrective to error, a very effective guide in action, and not by any means inconsistent with the conception of a loving, spiritual father.

Y. B. What about the cruelty of the natural world, of allowing one species to live upon another? The tooth and fang of the jungle.

M. There are things in the natural world, I admit, that are difficult for us with our finite powers of apprehension to reconcile with the conception of a God of compassionate love.

Y. B. Aren't you giving away your point? Isn't war extremely like the tooth and fang of the jungle?

M. Too much so to suit me. I hope I am one removed from the jungle. In any case I could not bring myself to commit the appalling atrocities that war demands.

Y. B. Supposing you were a young airman, couldn't you at least see the romance and excitement of it even though you were killing?

M. Could you?

Y. B. Thousands did.

M. Yes, but could you?

Y. B. (*laughing*) We are getting too personal. Do you admit that there are any righteous wars at all? For example would you admit that a war on the Indian Frontier might be justified?

M. I have yet to learn of a righteous war. As for the Indian Frontier, when Gandhi was in London I asked him how he would defend India from the tribesmen. He said he did not fear them; they were his kinsmen. Abdul Ghaffar Khan, the leader on the north-west Frontier, and his followers, had responded with whole-hearted friendliness to his appeal for non-violence. If their grievances were sympathetically considered the friendship of the hostile tribesmen could be won.

Y. B. I would like to take you up there on several points. I feel justified in doing so because I think I know more than Gandhi about the Indian Frontier. I have lived there which is more than he has done. I can speak the Afridi language and I am sure he cannot. I know the Afridi and I am sure he doesn't. You tell me he could find out the Afridi's grievances, ask them what was the matter. Do you know what the Afridis would reply? They would merely say, 'Our land is barren — we live by looting.'

That's what's the matter with them; they are poor. What is Gandhi going to do about that? What possible alternative would he have except a system of subsidies and armed force like that of the Indian Government?

M. The combination of threats and bribes seems a trifle unheroic to me somehow. It is often said that Orientals only understand force, that they only respect the strong hand. I seem to spot something of this attitude in what you are saying. If I may say so without offence, it is the philosophic basis of militarism, and not merely towards Orientals either. The reasoning is applied indiscriminately and at will to Russians, Germans, Irish, to strikers in our own streets, indeed to human beings in general. To my mind it is an utterly false conception. The 'stand no nonsense' attitude denotes intellectual cowardice and is most mischievous in its effects.

Y. B. My attitude is not that of the 'stand no nonsense' kind at all. I am very fond of the Afridis. Much fonder than Gandhi is, probably. The Afridis, if they were articulate, would say that all this talk of Truth and Love is mostly hypocrisy or degenerate twaddle: they respect the British because we have on the whole dealt fairly and justly with them. They wouldn't respect us if we couldn't or wouldn't safeguard the people living within our borders. Gandhi says he is not afraid of the Afridis. You must remember that he is living about a thousand miles away from the seat of the trouble.

M. Are you suggesting that Gandhi is a coward?

Y. B. Not at all. I am only suggesting that he hasn't seen women's hands cut off to remove their bangles and girls carried off to indescribable horrors. Gandhi has not seen an Afridi raiding party.

M. War always seems to transform otherwise decent people into madmen. I will not say into wild beasts for wild beasts behave more decently. Take Irishmen as one example. I can think of no people more lovable, more gentle, yet in the Irish Civil War — words fail to describe the horrors. War is so unnatural to men that it simply drives them mad. That you cannot 'cast out Beelzebub by Beelzebub' is also demonstrably true. Violence begets violence and leaves a legacy of sullen resentment. War settles nothing, except which is the more effectively vicious party to the dispute.

Y. B. Would you apply that to the savages in Africa?

M. Yes. First because 'savage' is not a fair or a gentlemanly epithet to apply to the African at home, and second because the attitude of the Africans towards Livingstone and all white men who have shown them friendliness, affords overwhelming evidence in favour of my contention.

Y. B. And for London as well? Would you abolish the police?

M. Police unarmed are stronger than police armed. Police carrying firearms are a definite danger. Courageous friendliness and fair treatment is the only way to bring out the good in men.

Y. B. I don't believe that courageous friendliness is enough to deal with the Indian tribes.

M. You think then that human nature is essentially evil?

Y. B. No! It isn't a question of human nature, it is merely that the Indian border tribes want more money and food than their land will yield.

M. Then the remedy is not force but food; that's the cure.

Y. B. Only part of the cure. The Indian Government is protecting defenceless people on the Frontier in the same way as the police are protecting us here in London.

M. If, as you say, these people are short of food, then it is no solution to pen them in on uncultivatable land. The British Government goes part way to recognize the position both on the Indian Frontier and in the industrial cities at home, by a system of doles, but in both cases the accompaniment of force makes the act ungracious and takes away any psychological value it might otherwise have had.

Y. B. Don't you believe the police in London are a protection?

M. In one sense of course I do, but I entirely dissent from the conventional idea that crime increases in inverse ratio with the number of police. Lawlessness springs from deep-seated causes which have to be understood and treated. All attempts to impose discipline by fear, and in this respect military and police methods are fundamentally the same, are wholly unsound in my opinion. I don't think the police are really such a protection as is usually made out.

Y. B. Well I happen to believe that they are. Without law and order no civilization is possible. There are rascals in every street, in Mayfair as much as in Whitechapel or in Peshawar.

M. I agree, but I also believe that they would yield to treatment.

Y. B. I don't, not to your treatment. You seem to me to deny the very basis of civilization. You might as well say that surgeons are wicked because they use their knives. Some surgeons may operate too much and some nations may use force too much as an instrument of policy; the Germans in 1914 for instance, and the Japanese to-day. But some force will always be necessary in human affairs. Armies and police are really the doctors of civilization, not its destroyers as you seem to think. Without them the rascals would get the upper hand.

M. But what constitutes a rascal? Isn't rascality mostly a question of balance? And do you suggest that your rascals are all rascal or only partially rascal? I submit that we are all potentially partial rascals, but that there is something essentially divine in us all, something that illumines, something that checks, something that keeps us in balance. This something under certain circumstances can be stifled, under other circumstances can be brought out on top. You seem to think that this something cannot be relied upon and that it is better to bring out the police!

III

M. As you know I am an absolutist, an extremist, the lunatic fringe, if you like, the wrecker of all good order. I have been dubbed worse things than that. My position is vulnerable, perhaps untenable, in a world built upon our present inequity.

Y. B. In other words you think that Communism is the solution?

M. I do not stand for any particular 'ism' or political creed, but for the life of me I cannot see why in material things people should not have everything they want. Actually or potentially it is there. In our human make-up are implanted an infinite variety of wants and at the same time an infinite variety of talents to cater for them, and of the wants the most urgent in normal beings is the desire, one might almost say the passionate desire, to love, to give, to serve, in any case to be usefully occupied, contriving, constructing, cultivating and exercising his talents. In other words, as you soldiers so fully appreciate, the call of 'active service' makes an irresistible appeal to normal men.

IV

Y. B. We are getting off the point. Let me ask you a question I asked you before. Why do you consider it so important that people should not lose their lives?

M. I don't. But I have a horror of taking life, indeed I would a hundred times rather be killed than kill.

Y. B. It wouldn't disturb me like that, I am too Oriental.

M. Honestly, I would much rather suffer death unjustly than take life in an apparently just cause.

Y. B. But why, man, why? A man's got to die sometime, why should he not die by being shot as by any other means? Surely to be shot is as good as dying of cancer or fatty degeneration of the heart. You must forgive me if

I seem to be putting a rather Chestertonian point of view to you, but it seems to me that there are so many wonderful things about life that war and death don't matter as much as liberty, progress, honour, adventure.

M. It isn't so much the ante-dating of the hour of death, it is the calculated callousness of war, the suppression of the natural instincts of compassion, in fact of the instincts of a gentleman. I remember a parson during the war saying to me, 'but we did expect the Germans to fight like gentlemen', to which I replied, 'Can you tell me how to stick a bayonet into a man like a gentleman?'

Y. B. It seems to me more gentlemanly to stick a bayonet into a man than to ruin him economically as Mr. Gandhi is ruining the cotton spinners of Lancashire.

M. I admit that our economic system is more subtle in its cruelty, but if you had seen Gandhi in Lancashire and heard him talk to the cotton operatives, you would have realized that he was trying to save them, not to ruin them. After all he came from Indian villages whose inhabitants had been made destitute by the importation of English cloth. He wanted to bring the workers of Lancashire into one great scheme of co-operation with the workers of India of which the animating principle was love.

Y. B. But that wasn't much help to the weavers. You pacifists have a material view of love. God is love, but God chastises those He loves on due occasions, and to their great benefit. We mustn't think of love as being always peace. I can see myself loving a man and hitting him as hard as I can on the nose. There is a time to fight and a time to refrain from fighting. Supposing you were a Hungarian, supposing your country had been chopped about and mutilated with artificial boundaries ruled through it by foreign powers. What would you do?

M. All this the legacy of war, remember! I suppose your idea is that another little war wouldn't do them any harm. Do you seriously suggest that such problems can be solved by the ruthless arbitrament of war? Who is to say that the Hungarian might not lose still more of his lands?

Y. B. You haven't answered my question. What would you do?

M. I should try to get the parties to study the problem in a friendly spirit on the spot, or better still from an aeroplane. There is nothing like a bird's-eye view of Europe to demonstrate how artificial and imaginary national frontiers are.

Y. B. I think you are over-optimistic about getting the parties to a quarrel to study the problem in a friendly spirit on the spot. You mustn't shirk the fact that they probably won't agree, even in an aeroplane. Frontiers aren't at all imaginary; you think they are, because you live on this safe little island, but to the Hungarian or German they are real enough. Supposing you were like a Hungarian I have heard of, who has had the Rumanian frontier ruled right through his estate, so that while his house is still in Hungary his family mausoleum is in Rumania. What would you say if you couldn't put flowers on your mother's grave without asking the permission of a foreign sentry?

M. Even if my proposals for a friendly compromise

were continually and persistently rejected, I should certainly not advocate another war to rectify matters, and incidentally add to the number of occupants of the family mausoleum! One doesn't use a crowbar to mend a watch. Problems of this kind require dispassionate friendliness for their solution. War immediately creates passionate enmity. Let me make my position clear. I should definitely say that there will be cases for nations as for individuals where the true heroism is to suffer wrong without retaliation, without even bitterness of heart, but as I tried to make clear in the beginning of our discussion, this would not mean mere passivism, rather an unceasing, active pacifism.

Y. B. Then if everybody had always suffered wrong without retaliation the most savage men and nations of the world would now be the rulers of it, and the idealists would be their slaves. I don't call that a 'truly heroic' state of affairs at all. Wouldn't you fight for the world of your ideals?

M. I should not use means which were wholly inconsistent with those ideals, as war would be.

Y. B. Wouldn't you use a revolver on your fellow men under any circumstances?

M. No. For anyone setting to work in the way and in the spirit that I have indicated it would obviously be a grand mistake to have arms about his person. Such would lay him immediately under suspicion and defeat his end.

Y. B. Have you ever lived in a lawless city, for example in Peshawar?

M. No, but it is a fact that throughout the terrible Irish rebellion of 1845 Quakers in the most lawless districts made no effort to defend themselves, did not even lock their doors, and no harm befell a single one of them. Eagerly and actively they concentrated their efforts on pacifying both sides, and I venture to think that their quiet calm courage was more effective than all the forces of so-called law and order.

V

Y. B. Do you really believe that a world of pacifism would be a world of progress?

M. Most assuredly. A world in which 'active service' meant not destruction but construction, where the resourcefulness of men was used to exploit not human beings but natural wealth, such a world would progress at an unheard of rate and it certainly would lack neither colour nor adventure. There is unlimited scope in a world without war for courage, daring and enterprise at every turn.

Y. B. Yes, there is theoretically. But practically the sense of friendship which existed between all classes during the war (and say what you will it did exist) has not survived into this post-war age, nor has heroism on any large scale. It should have, but it hasn't. Only a few daring spirits can succeed in the adventures of peace. I must admit that we ought to be able to find much better things to do than fighting each other, yet I am inclined to agree with Ruskin, who wrote that all the greatest qualities of man come out in armed conflict. Ruskin was horrified by this discovery but he didn't shirk the truth when it didn't agree with his theories, as we are all inclined to do. I think we are inclined to exaggerate, to become hysterical when we discuss war. Some of us who write and talk about it might be psycho-analysed with advantage to discover whether our opinions are based on cold reason or are due to repressions and complexes. I don't know. I admit I don't see clearly myself, but I question a great many of the slick assertions of the pacifists. It seems to me that the French are logical when they say that if we really want world peace we must have a world police, and do we want a world police? I will keep an open mind on that until it becomes practical politics. It might be a good thing, but it would make any kind of progress rather difficult, for the world controllers would inevitably become a bureaucracy jealous of their own rights and prestige.

M. You have mentioned Ruskin. It was he who said of human nature: 'Thinking it high, I have always found it higher than I thought it, while whose who think it low, find it and will always find it, lower than they thought it.' Before we can plan economic or political life aright, for our own nation or for the world, we must have more of this faith in the uncommon fineness of the common man.

Y. B. Nobody knows better than the soldier of the uncommon fineness of the common man. And the common man is not a pacifist, thank God!

AUTHOR'S NOTE

I do not wish to extend an argument which is already exhaustive, and might tend to become exhausting, but I cannot refrain from pointing out to Messrs. Mennel and

Yeats Brown that they both seem to be labouring under a confusion of thought in one important aspect of the discussion, i.e. they both confuse the 'police' with the 'army'.

The police and the army have exactly *contrary* functions. The object of an army is to enable the litigant to be also his own judge. The object of a police force is to *prevent* the litigant from being his own judge. This is a really vital distinction, which is often overlooked even by supporters of the League of Nations.

I would also suggest to Yeats Brown, when he refers to an army as a means of 'defence', that he should be quite clear as to what he means by the word. Certainly he cannot mean defence of the soil. If he does, he is forced into the invidious position of admitting that his own country must have pursued a singularly offensive policy, throughout history, in view of the fact that the British army has fought *in almost every country in the world except Greenland!*

CHAPTER XIII

THE ROOT OF ALL EVIL?

WHATEVER else the last chapter did for you, I hope it made you think. It certainly had that effect on me. I need hardly say that, although many of Yeats Brown's sallies went home, my main conviction, at the end of the dialogue was overwhelmingly in favour of Mennel. And strangely enough, the few sentences of his which, in retrospect, most impressed me were those which brought from Yeats Brown the reproof that he was 'getting off the point'. It seemed to me that this was the precise moment where Mennel was getting *on* the point. If you are interested, perhaps you would turn back and look at section III of the last chapter. Or if that is too much bother, here are the words to which I refer:

'My position is vulnerable, perhaps untenable, in a world built upon our present inequity. I do not stand for any particular "ism" or political creed, but for the life of me I cannot see why in material things people should not have everything they want. Actually or potentially it is there. In our human make-up are implanted an infinite variety of wants and at the same time an infinite variety of talents to cater for them, and of the wants the most urgent in normal beings is the desire, one might almost say the passionate desire, to love, to give, to serve, in any case to be usefully occupied, contriving, constructing, cultivating and exercising his talents.'

Those are not really vague words, though it is true that they might be more definite. They hover over the very centre of the problem. And though Yeats Brown's query 'Is Communism the solution?' was perhaps a rather brusque way of pinning Mennel down, it was so obviously a question that had to be asked, sooner of later, that I am glad he asked it.

'Is Communism the solution?'

I thought and thought over that question, and once more, I became addle-headed. 'This is another occasion for calling in outside help,' I said to myself. 'The question to be decided is:

'IS PEACE POSSIBLE UNDER CAPITALISM?'

'Obviously, we must have another dinner party.'

And so I racked my brains to think of the most intelligent advocate of Socialism. . . . (I know all about the difference between socialism and communism, but we need not go into that now) . . . and the most intelligent advocate of Capitalism. Finally I decided that I could not find any pair more suitably matched than Mr. G. D. H. Cole and Sir Arthur Salter. If these names do not mean anything to you, you will find a sober list of their achievements in *Who's Who*, which will be more impressive than any eulogies I could offer.

Anyway I asked these two men to dinner, and they both came, and this is what they said:

SIR ARTHUR. My position is that peace can be maintained under capitalism on certain conditions. One vital condition for example is that no section of the capitalist system shall be allowed to get into a position in which it can dictate *public policy*.

This danger exists in the case of the armaments business. The principal armaments makers are concentrated in a few great companies: The Bethlehem Steel Company in America, Vickers Armstrong in England, Schneider-Creusot in France, Skoda in Czecho-Slovakia and Mitsui in Japan. Their strength makes it possible for them to influence public opinion and political action very powerfully. Their financial interest is obviously that there should be a general state of anxiety which increases the demand for munitions. I believe the only solution is that the private manfacture of arms should be prohibited.

I realize that there are great difficulties. For example non-manufacturing countries are accustomed to buy from one or other of the above firms. If these no longer remain as private companies they would have to buy from the governments, and that would involve more definite political responsibilities.

COLE. Wouldn't that establish an even more powerful dictatorship of the great powers?

S. I don't know that the position would in this respect be substantially changed. Control of the export of arms is already exercised by licence; and the countries with big armament industries are already in a position to dictate.

C. Yes, but wouldn't your system lead direct to the arming of vassal states? In the same manner as Poland has now been armed by France?

S. It would scarcely increase this tendency. But I should like to see the prohibition of the private manufacture of arms accompanied by an international convention limiting peace armaments and providing that any country fighting with League approval — that is a victim of aggression — would be able to obtain arms freely.

C. If you had this system wouldn't it mean that you would have alliances and counter alliances of nations — the old conception of the balance of power?

S. You've got it now.

C. But you would have to use it in a form which would lead still more to the subjection of the small nations, if they could only arm by getting their arms from the national enterprises of the Great Powers.

S. Not if the League functions as it was intended to.

C. But will it? Of course, the League *can* act as an organ of publicity, which I admit is an advantage.

S. Anyway I think we are both agreed that the world must free itself from the poisonous influence of armament interests. As things are at the moment, one does not know how far the secret understandings stretch. One has no idea of their ramifications.

C. How much hope have you that this can actually be done?

S. I will tell you that later. All I will say for the moment is that if we cannot do it, we are lost.

II

I asked Cole to explain the reason for his distrust of the League of Nations as an effective body, especially as he had admitted its value as an organ of publicity.

c. I agree that the League is a useful organ of publicity. But I also consider it to be an organ of delay. It takes too long to get the machinery in motion, and any interested objector can hold it up until it is too late.

s. The League is what we make it. All the League can do is to give to the forces of peace the best possible chance for maintaining peace. It cannot go beyond that.

c. All the same, if you take a concrete example like the Chinese-Japanese dispute, I think it is quite arguable that America might have acted more effectively if the League of Nations had not been in existence.

I can imagine a consortium of powers which might have acted more quickly than the League.

s. But you would not have had a consortium. You would have had a *competition* of powers. For example, before the League of Nations, the Manchurian question would have been a signal for all the powers to have begun fishing in troubled waters. Now, they have united, even if their union has been ineffective. I agree that it *has* been ineffective, but at least there has not been competitive looting.

I might sum up this point by saying that in pre-League days the great powers were competitive burglars. Now they are collective policemen. The fact that they always showed much more enthusiasm in the first role than they have in the second is no argument for suggesting that they should return to their old trade.

c. But even supposing the League *had* taken its courage in both hands, and decided to enforce penalties against Japan, were any countries going to risk the expenditure of arms and men which such a decision would have involved?

s. I think the risk would have been remote. If the world had shown that it was united and determined, and prepared if necessary to act for example by the exclusion of Japanese imports, I believe that Japan would have modified her policy.

c. Yes, I agree — if it had been done eighteen months ago. Which brings us back to the dilatory procedure of the League.

s. To the dilatory behaviour of the governments concerned. There was no delay in Geneva. The delay was in the world capitals.

c. But surely procedure under the League is a matter of investigation and report, with a maximum power to delay action?

s. No. Look at the time table of 1925.

c. In the dispute between Greece and Bulgaria?

s. Yes, we learnt of the outbreak of hostilities on Friday morning. We sent a warning that same morning. Hostilities were stopped at once. On Monday we had a Meeting of the Council. On Tuesday British, French, and Italian military officers had arrived by aeroplane from Athens.

c. Yes — Greece and Bulgaria! *Not Great Powers!* I don't believe that the great powers would submit to such procedure. Mind you, I have no objection to the League. I would rather it was there than it wasn't. But I still maintain that it cannot be a reality until we have transcended the national antagonisms between the countries which compose it. I also think that as the world is to-day, the League cannot be a reality without American co-operation. I think on this very important Japanese question the League did act as a delaying instrument, and we have no guarantee that it will not act in a similarly disastrous way again.

III

As this argument tended to go off into side-issues I asked Mr. Cole to explain, as briefly as possible, why he thought peace was more likely under socialism than under capitalism. After a natural objection that such an argument, to be convincing, would need about a quarter of a million words for its development, he smiled, lit a cigarette, and spoke as follows:

'When I study the capitalist world to-day, I am driven to the conclusion that capitalist society is finding it impossible to continue on the basis of increasing production, finding new markets, overseas investments as it was doing in the nineteenth century.

'The logical conclusion of the present situation seems to be that capitalism, having exhausted all the available markets of the world, will be forced to attempt the economic exploitation of the moon! Isn't it fairly obvious that this must lead to strife? When societies are brought more and more into competition with one another in the development of unexploited parts of the world, when, in addition, they find it more and more difficult to distribute income, on a wide enough basis to provide an outlet for the growth of the world's productive power, it follows as clearly as night follows day that they are forced to develop their imperialist tendencies to the fullest extent.

'What happens? Fewer and fewer of the more pressing reforms can be granted in any country, however democratic, because of this pressure of international competition. *But*, as capitalism can only hope to survive with the aid of some sort of democratic appeal, it turns the attempt to play on popular nationalist passions as an alternative to class appeal. This in its turn gives rise to Fascism, for example, the present regime in Germany.

'I cannot see a permanent cure for this situation under capitalism, even under concerted national capitalism. It may be quite true that reinflation might temporarily cure some of the greater ills. But we should head back and inevitably to another imperialistic crash. Which, of course, would involve the complete breakdown of capitalism.

'That is the first part of my argument. The second, and more difficult, is to prove that socialism is more compatible with peace than capitalism.

'I would preface my remarks by saying that I am not an orthodox Marxian, as some people understand Marxism, because I do not believe that socialism must inevitably follow the breakdown of capitalism. I believe that it would be perfectly possible for capitalism to collapse without socialism taking its place. If socialism were to develop on national lines, so that we should have the growth of a bastard socialism in each country, entirely independent of its growth in other countries, I do not believe that this sort of socialism would overcome our troubles.

'That is the idea I would like to put into the minds of people with whom I come into contact. I feel we have reached a position where we have to say to ourselves, "I don't care what happens to my country. I care only for socialism in the world as a whole."

'I am not interested in working for socialism in any other sense than this. I am not interested in the nationalization of industry in England, for its own sake, or in a purely national victory for the Labour Party here. I would rather not get votes for socialism at all than get them for a bastard national socialism. And that is what I am really afraid of—that socialism may be called to power while it is still permeated with nationalism.

'Perhaps instead of "international" I ought to have been using the word "cosmopolitan", because that expresses the sort of socialism I want far more accurately. I feel that we must deny in our own minds that there are such things as nations at all as bodies entitled to claim our final loyalty. I really do feel that if, for example, China is in need of any commodity, we should give these commodities to China whether she is in a position to pay for them or not.'

S. In other words make them a gift?

C. Exactly.

S. And is that your case for peace under Socialism?

C. As far as it is possible to make out a case after a good dinner, on the spur of the moment! If you like I will sum it up. And I would say, with deep conviction, that *as long as you have capitalist interests in each nation trying to get profits for themselves, you are going to have wars.* Wars are, I believe, bound to happen as long as exploitation continues to be the basis of the economic system. Whereas, if each country really were organized in a classless society, and really had got rid of its own profiteers, there would be no valid reason for one country to quarrel with another. I admit there would still remain the possibility that the developed countries would try to exploit the less developed, but I hold that the chief motive for doing this would disappear as soon as there ceased to be any difficulty of finding a market in consumption for everything that could be produced. That would necessarily be the position in a socialist society. And, with socialism, the motive which drives states towards imperialism would be so weakened as to be easily capable of international control, even if it did not, as I think it would, vanish altogether.

IV

s. Well, you have given me something to answer. I will endeavour to do so. But remember, I am speaking on the spur of the moment, too, and I ate the same dinner as you!

Sir Arthur Salter's Case.

s. I won't answer you directly. I want to suggest that there are four possible systems, two of them capitalist and two of them socialist. Under two of these four (one capitalist, one socialist) I believe that peace can be preserved. Under the other two I believe that it cannot be preserved.

Here is my first system. It is a capitalist system in

which the relations between government and private interests are firmly established on a proper basis. Internally in each country the political situation is such that no private interest (such as oil or armaments) can prevail over the public interest and dominate public policy. Externally the different governments agree upon the limits to their respective action in helping or hindering the competition of their nationals for world trade.

This doesn't involve anything so drastic as the abolition of all tariffs. If a country decides to give an advantage in its home market to its own industrialists, that may be economically unwise, but it should not in itself be a cause of serious quarrels with other countries. Of course if changes are made abruptly, so that foreign interests are suddenly and seriously prejudiced, there will be friction. But what the interests of peace require is really only provision for a reasonable stability in tariffs. Subsidies to exporters, however, are on a very different footing. They are much more provocative than tariffs, because the government which gives them is not acting in its own national market, but making a raid (with the aid of public funds compulsorily raised in taxation) upon the general world market, which is no more theirs than anyone else's. International agreement to limit governmental subsidies for export is therefore of great importance. Thirdly, agreement is needed as to the conditions of export and import in the case of a dependent, non-self-governing Empire. The 'open door', or the 'equality of treatment' provided in the mandates of the ex-German colonies in Central Africa are the safest principles.

If the capitalist system could satisfy these three

conditions, it could to my mind continue indefinitely without threatening peace. Of course there would be trade quarrels between competing enterprises. But they would be the quarrels of individuals not of states; they would not affect the relations of whole peoples. In contrast with this, if you have a socialist state competing with other similar states, or (more probably and even worse) one socialist state competing with private enterprises in other states, quarrels are much more dangerous, because they involve the action of governments and the reactions of whole countries. You then have the irresponsibilities of private quarrelling combined with the immense powers and forces involved in public quarrelling.

c. How does this apply to Colonial Empires?

s. I agree that the Ottawa Conference marked a serious further step in the direction of a 'closed' dependent Empire. The only safe principle in any large Empire is that of the open door and equality of opportunity. The British Empire used to be open to all countries . . .

c. It isn't now.

s. No. And this may ultimately endanger the peace of the world. However, let us stick to the point.

That is my first system. I regard it as safer than any form of socialism because it would be subject to a framework of law in which the quarrels of individuals would remain the quarrels of individuals, and would not involve positive action by governments.

c. If I might interrupt, I would suggest that the policy of the open door was never true of any other Empire than ours.

s. It was true of the Dutch.

C. But never of the French. I very much doubt if the idea of an open Colonial Empire is practical in the twentieth century. As competitive pressure increases in great imperialistic powers, the closed door seems to be the inevitable outcome.

S. If that is so, then the danger of war arising from the possession of a dependent Empire is greatly increased, but I do not agree that it is so.

C. Well, we have begun with Ottawa. And now the French are going to follow our example with a Colonial League Conference of their own. What I really want to say is this, that the vision that you have just painted is a vision of an effete Cobdenism.

S. I agree that the movement has recently been in the opposite direction to the one I wish. But this is very recently; and the movement may be reversed.

C. But I think the very possibility of that sort of *laisser-faire*, open-door, imperial capitalism, stopped when capitalism developed from the selling of shirts to the construction of railways—i.e. when governments were forced to intervene in political affairs. When you sell a man a shirt, you don't care what he does with it. When you sell him a railway, you have to, because he can only pay by instalments, or you stand over him with a gun to see that he is well behaved, and does go on paying.

S. Let me come to my second system. It is the system of socialism which I think would *not* tend to peace.

I regret to say that this sort of socialism, which I fear, is just the one that is likely to come. It will be a national and bastard socialism. It will be bastard because it will not be planned by real socialists but will come as a result of yielding to the demands of what I might call capitalist socialisticism — the demand by an organized private interest for a form of state control which will increase their own powers of exploitation.

c. I am strongly opposed to socialiticism!

s. I think this form of socialism would be dangerous because it would involve the whole people in each economic quarrel. If the coal industry were nationalized in that way, and if it had the whole power of the state behind it, and if, for example, we were trying to wrest the iron market from Sweden, such a quarrel, which under the present system would be a quarrel of individuals, would become a quarrel of the whole nation.

c. To which I should reply '*Corruptio optimi pessima*.'

s. Now for the third system, that is your own form of socialism, which grows up on an international basis. I agree that under all your ideal conditions, you would have a system compatible with peace. My objection is not that such a form of socialism would endanger peace; but that it is not the kind of socialism that is coming, and that it is not practicable. Difficult as it is to get my three conditions, it would be immensely more difficult to get yours, because your system implies an evenness of development over a very large part of the world which is animated by many conflicting ideals.

Apart from that, it seems to me that you are implying motives which are as illusory as those of William Morris in his Utopia, where man works to give and takes no care about his reward.

I cannot see Morris's Utopia in our world. And therefore, I cannot see your Utopia either. I cannot for example visualize a society where Great Britain would send £10,000,000 worth of cotton to China without recompense or any expectation of recompense. I have been within an ace of seeing my 'ideal system'. You are not within a hundred years of seeing yours.

My fourth system can be described in a very few words. Unhappily it is the system which on the whole tends to prevail to-day, If armaments interests are allowed to dominate public policy, if the Empire is to be closed, and if it is impossible to restrain governments from the competitive subsidizing of private enterprise in world markets, we are likely to have war and world chaos. But this existing system can be more easily transformed into my ideal system than yours.

C. I would like to take you up on several points in your first system, your ideal capitalism. Because I believe that even if all your conditions were realized, they would not necessarily establish peace. Even supposing you could limit capitalism so that it would be forced to abide by national rules, it would break down because of its inability to distribute in each society the resources of its production.

S. I don't follow you.

C. The system of capitalist production leaves you with a supply of goods which, obviously, you can produce, but which you cannot market at home. The system leads inevitably to a surplus of saving among a large section of the community. And saving is valueless without an extension of consuming power. And obviously you cannot extend consuming power indefinitely.

S. Why not? To simplify the argument let us

imagine a self-sufficient state—the United States for example, ringed round and completely shut off from the rest of the world. You would naturally have an accumulation of saving. What would happen? The return on capital would go down and down until a half per cent would be a very high rate of interest. In this and other ways surplus saving would spread out indefinitely with it because of correspondingly increased purchasing power and therefore consuming demand.

c. I think you are making an unjustified assumption by suggesting a series of isolated economic systems. Isn't it impossible? However, let us go on to your second assumption. If you assume an isolated economy, you obviously assume a drive to economic nationalism and national socialism. You don't get stable capitalism.

And with regard to the third system . . . my system. I agree that men won't be socialists until it has been definitely proved that capitalism will not work. I wouldn't myself hope to establish socialism if I thought that capitalism could be made a going concern. But I think that history proves that it has worked only under exceptional circumstances. It worked for Great Britain during the industrial revolution. It worked for America while America was still undeveloped. Where are we to find any set of circumstances in any country even vaguely resembling the circumstances which produced the heyday of capitalism? I have definitely given up hope of rescuing the capitalist world from chaos. You haven't. You say that your ideal system was within an ace of realization. I say that *my* system was nearly realized.

s. *When?*

c. In 1919. If the German social democrats and the British socialists had known how to use their chances then, we could have had the real beginning of a system of international socialism.

The argument ended with these characteristic observations:

c. I feel the fundamental difference between us is that I feel instinctively that economic equality is *right*.

s. I do not know that I would agree that absolute equality of income is desirable. But my ideal society would be based upon a certain fundamental personal and social equality. It would recognize differences in quality, and an ability that would not exaggerate them or add to them — there would be the kind of equality which existed, say, between the late Lord Balfour and the most stupid member of his family.

c. The kind of equality I want is a civilization where I can ask my cook in to dinner without her feeling more uncomfortable than I do.

CHAPTER XIV

THE MICROBES OF MARS

AND now, it would seem, it is time for the author to sum up. The plan of this little book is as complete as it is ever likely to be. We can put a tick against Part one (offence), Part two (defence), and Part three (existing organizations for peace). And Part four, by means of dialogue, has surely given us enough material to enable us to make up our minds? We don't want to call in any more help, do we? We can, if you like, but I do not think it will get us much further.

Therefore, I suppose I *should* sum up.

Yet — if you look back on the journey we have taken together, you will see that there is one very big gap in the winding road of argument. How we missed it, I really do not know, but miss it we did, and it is essential that we should retrace our steps, even at the risk of fatigue. For while we have been talking about war, what it will be like, what horrors it will bring in its train, what efforts are being made to avert it, whether it is intrinsically evil or intrinsically good, we have not really asked ourselves the question '*What is War's Ultimate Cause?*'

Why do men fight, when they would much prefer to live at peace? *Why* do nations pour out their treasure in destruction when they sorely need it for construction? *Why* do people deliberately choose the disease of war when they might choose the radiant health of peace? You cannot explain these monstrous paradoxes merely by attributing them to the sinister activities of armament firms. You cannot put all the blame on the press, nor can you talk vaguely about men's 'instincts'. We want a clearer diagnosis than that. We want an absolutely conclusive answer to the question 'What are the microbes of Mars?'

Now, do you see the meaning of the somewhat lurid title of this chapter? It sounds like an Edgar Wallace thriller but really it is as apposite a title as you could choose. For unless we make a scientific diagnosis there is a grave danger that we shall go grievously astray.

This bacteriological examination which we are about to make should, of course, have come at the beginning instead of the end. However, it is too late to alter it now. And perhaps it is just as well that the most important part of the book should come at the end. For make no mistake about it, this diagnosis *is* the most important part of the book, for the microbes of Mars are as cunning as the pale spirochetes of syphilis, as deep rooted, and as difficult to eradicate. Moreover, the same damnable prudery and superstition thwarts the efforts of those who wish to destroy them. The man who talks openly and sensibly about these microbes will be regarded, by many respectable people, with as much distaste as the man who talks openly and sensibly about syphilis.

I must risk that. I think the father who does not acquaint himself with the peculiarities of the most insidious of man's diseases, its symptoms and its treatment, in order to pass on this information to his son, is not only a fool but a criminal. However, I would not give him so hard a sentence as the man who deliberately infects his son with the microbes of Mars.

If you are a father, can you honestly deny that you have infected your son in this way?

However, you can't answer that question till you know what the microbes are. We will therefore proceed to our diagnosis. I warn you that it will be a painful process for both of us. For the generic name of all these poisonous germs which cause war is . . . Patriotism.

There was once a great and noble Englishwoman who cried, in her last hours . . . 'Patriotism is not enough!' As long as fine deeds are commemorated, her words will ring in the hearts of decent men. But now, those who have courage and faith must be prepared to deny them. They must be prepared to face the scorn and hatred of their fellows by denying their birthright.

I have put the case in its extreme and most 'shocking' aspect because I believe, with every fibre of my being, that the hour has struck in the world's history when every man who wishes to serve his country must realize that Patriotism is the worst service he can offer to it. The time has come when it must be definitely admitted that Patriotism is an Evil, in every country — that the German patriot is as great a sinner as the English patriot or the American patriot or the Italian patriot. The time has come when this word — a hallowed word, I admit, a word that calls up memories of sublime sacrifice and deathless heroism — must be recognized as having changed its meaning, and as having lost its sense and its virtue.

II

It will be a difficult task, for me as well as for you. I was brought up in a conservative English household, with no sort of eccentricities, and I believed everything I was told in the war. Such influences are not easily forgotten. They are not forgotten yet. It is only the force of overwhelming conviction that makes me compel myself to define this word as it really is.

Now the first thing to realize about patriotism is that it is *not* an 'instinct'. We are brought up — most of us — to imagine that it is a quality with which every decent man is born — that if, when the child becomes adolescent it does not show the usual signs of 'patriotism', there is something wrong with the child.

This is such an obvious fallacy that it seems hardly worthy of refutation. However, a very simple example will serve to refute it. Take a German baby, a French baby and an American baby, at the age of six months, and transport those babies to a little island in the Pacific. What are they then? They are helpless creatures dependent on you, and on you alone. They are certainly not 'patriots'. They never will be patriots, unless you make them so. And supposing you are an Englishman, in charge of those babies, and you only speak English, and you bring them all up to speak English too, will you regard the German baby and the French baby as 'unnatural' because they do not leap about the island crying 'Deutschland uber Alles' or 'Vive la France?'

These are ludicrous and puerile suppositions, are they not? Yes? Very well then. It is also ludicrous and puerile to suppose that patriotism is 'instinctive'. It is utterly artificial. A product of education only. So far we are at one.

But before we go on any further, I think it will be worth our while to examine the *reason* why quite intelligent men still couple the words 'patriotism' and 'instinct'. I believe that it is largely because of a very simple verbal confusion. Every nation *personifies* itself. We talk of 'Mother England'. The Germans talk of the 'Fatherland'. The Italians, the French, the Americans, the Turks, the Chinese, and almost every other existent nation, adopt the same odd conceit. I call it 'odd' because it *is* odd, this confusion of a blood relationship with an accident of geography. The boundaries of many nations are the result of pure caprice, the consequence of a turn in the political wheel, or the proverbial loss of a nail in a horse's shoe. And yet, because of this completely artificial, and frequently sordid, chapter of accidents which decides the limits of national territory, millions of men are trained, from infancy, to regard a strip of land as sacredly as they regard their 'mother'.

This seems to me, I repeat, odd. Indeed, it seems more than odd. It seems barbaric. Blood of my blood, flesh of my flesh . . . Yes, I understand that. As long as man is born of woman, he will venerate and cherish and protect the woman who gave him breath. Systems may rise and fall, and the stars of Empires may be lost in dusty confusion, but this, the most radiant love, will remain. And it seems to me an insult to mother love to confuse it with the entirely artificial mixture of fears, prejudices and superstitions which go to form the concept of 'patriotism'.

III

Now you say to me 'I am proud of being English.' (Or American, or German, or whatever it may be.) You say it absolutely sincerely, looking me straight in the eyes. And I answer you in the same spirit, absolutely sincerely, looking you straight in the eyes. And I say to you:

'Why?'

If our argument together is a serious one, if you are as earnest as I am, you will please try to answer that question:

'Why?'

You find some difficulty in answering it? You find none at all? You have a great many reasons, which you can write on a sheet of notepaper, to give me, explaining why you are proud to be English? Splendid! But before you begin to write, let me make a brief suggestion.

Pride comes from *achievement*, doesn't it? I am sure we are agreed about that. In case the generalization sounds too vague, let me put it in another way. Let me merely suggest that you will agree when I say that a man has no right to be proud of something which he has not *done*. A man of course, can be *grateful* for what he is . . . he can be grateful, to God, for inheriting riches, or inheriting health, or inheriting good looks . . . but I hope it will be generally agreed that a man should not be *proud* of inherited wealth, nor should he be *proud* of a perfect profile. If he is, we generally regard him as a snob or a bounder. Do we not? I think you will be with me — even if reluctantly — up to this point in the argument.

Well, then, why are you 'proud of being English?' Is not the answer to that — the only true answer — 'I am proud of the accident of being born in a certain bedroom?' Is there any other answer? And if there is not, is it an answer which you are so very proud of giving?

Please do not mistake me. Do not say 'but I am proud of *England* . . . apart from all that . . . proud of belonging to the land of Shakespeare and Shelley and Nelson.' That has nothing to do with it. We are not discussing the merits of particular nations. We are discussing an accident . . . an accident of birth. Are you *proud* of that accident? I do not see how you can be proud of an accident. Grateful, if you like, but surely not proud?

Since this is a new and strange and probably antipathetic form of reasoning to most readers, it is necessary to reiterate the difference between being proud of *England* and being proud of being *English*. This difference is really radical. I am as proud as any man to think that any strip of this tormented planet could produce a man like Shakespeare, whose starry words will always sparkle on the world's pages, as long as there is a wind to ruffle them. But I am surely permitted to say that I am equally proud of Germany? From Germany came Beethoven, to whom — if we are being personal — I owe a greater debt of ecstasy than to Shakespeare himself. And am I not also permitted to say that I am proud of Italy?

But, you tell me, the thing is deeper than that. Beyond reason. It is an emotional quality. You are impatient. You say to me:

How can I help loving England? England with the quiet lawns and the great trees in which the rooks are always restless, England whose summer is eternal April, whose winter is a sleep broken with distant laughter? How can I help loving this land of the grey cities and the grey sea, this land whose very reserve makes my loyalty more ardent? Even when I am far from England, under the blazing sun in some strange city of towers and temples, the thought of England shines more radiantly than the gold on any worshipped idol. I love its kings and its queens, its flags and its songs, and to me my English passport is itself a title of nobility.

You think that *you* were asking those questions, and that I was preparing to deliver some rhetorical snub? No. Those questions came from my own heart. Which shows how intensely difficult it is to eradicate them. Why should I wish to eradicate them, then? I don't. I only wish to clear them up and to eradicate the ridiculous tailpiece at the end of the paragraph — 'to me my English passport is itself a title of nobility'.

That is pure snobbery, of the most dangerous sort. National snobbery leads to war as clearly as social snobbery leads to revolution. My English passport is a matter of good luck, that is all. (At the moment of writing, I mean. By the time these words are published it may not be a matter of good luck at all.)

'But those pretty words of yours about England — didn't you mean them?' Certainly. As clearly as any pretty words I might write about Italy or France or

Japan. It is fatal to be exclusive about love of your country. If you say that it would be as difficult for you to love the whole world as it would be to love sixty women at once, my only answer is that you must try to do so. It is incredibly difficult. So is Christianity, which is all that I am advocating. It is the most difficult philosophy in the world, which is, presumably, the reason why it has never been tried.

For, make no mistake about it . . . this 'exclusive' love of yours will one day be the cause of destroying England. It will lead you to hate any other lovers of their countries. You will both fight for what you love, and you will both be destroyed. For as we have seen, earlier in this book, a new war will lay bare the nations with no respect of persons, no distinction between victors and vanquished. The English manor house will fall with the German castle and the Venetian palazzo and the Turkish mosque and the Russian factory. And they will fall because their owners loved them not wisely but too well.

IV

I am advocating a complete revolution in international thought. It sounds a somewhat ambitious programme. Actually this revolution could be accomplished in a single generation, by the simplest means, and without a pennyworth of expenditure.

However, you may say to me: 'You want a revolution in *international* thought. There's the snag! What is the use of *our* trying to be internationally-minded if the other nations are being as national as ever? What is the use of a few Englishmen trying to love their neighbours when their neighbours love only themselves?'

There are several answers to these questions. Firstly, you make a grave mistake if you imagine that the other nations are as 'national' as ever. There are tremendous international movements, largely suppressed, in every country of the world. Naturally, you do not hear much about them. The Italian press is completely gagged. The French press is largely under the control of armament manufacturers. At the moment of writing, every liberal paper in Germany has a soldier sitting on its editor's desk. But in all my European travels, which have been considerable in the past few years, I have found overwhelming evidence of a vast body of young international pacifism — disorganized, persecuted cruelly, hushed up, disgraced — but smouldering with intense activity. So we really are not quite so isolated as you may imagine, we pacifists.

Secondly, in reply to your objection that it is no use for an Englishman to be actively pacifist in a world which — I admit — contains a tremendous amount of red hot nationalism, I would reply that this argument of yours can be used in support of any form of cowardice or immorality you may like to mention. It would be exactly the same argument if you said to me 'What is the use of my trying to be a Christian in a world which contains so much evil?' You may answer that question for yourself.

Thirdly, and most important of all, one pacifist creates another. The reaction is international. If America builds an extra battleship, we feel that we must do the same. If she scraps a battleship, we relax. The force of example is incalculable. If, when you go out to dinner, you have the courage to answer some misguided man who, in a ruined world, and with the lesson of centuries of failure unlearnt, still maintains that 'we must prepare for war in order to obtain peace', if you can show him his tragic error, at the risk of losing his friendship, you will have done the best day's work you ever did.

Having made this general survey, we can now make a more detailed examination of the microbes which cause war. It will be fitting if we begin at the beginning, and go upstairs to the nursery.

V

If you are acquainted with the trend of modern psychological research, there will be no need to remind you of the startling experiments which Professor Pavlov has carried out in the effort to 'condition' the infant mind. These experiments formed the basis of a brilliant romantic conception which was presented to us by Mr. Aldous Huxley in his last novel *Brave New World*. Since Mr. Huxley is more picturesque than Professor Pavlov, and is certainly, in all essentials, as scientifically precise, we might do worse than refresh our memories of those last pages of *Brave New World*. They will give us an idea.

Mr. Huxley imagines a future world which has accepted the Aristotelean premise that society requires a slave basis for its efficient functioning. Whether this is true or not, we are as yet unaware. Perhaps we shall never learn the answer from man, perhaps we shall have to wait till it roars at us, suddenly, from the hoarse throat of a great machine. It does not matter, for the purposes of our present argument, which is only concerned with the *manufacture*, by the state, of a class with slave mentalities. This, Mr. Huxley suggests, is perfectly possible. He is probably right.

True, the beginning of his suggested treatment is still beyond us. We cannot affect the embryo . . . much. We cannot alter, with any degree of certainty, the mental tissues and the glandular structure of the unborn. But just bring back your mind, for one moment, to the things which are done to those babies when they *are* born, in order to ensure their servility.

Night after night they go to sleep to the crooning of gramophones which proclaim 'I'm glad I am a slave . . . I'm glad I am a slave!' All through their sleep this influence is at work, moulding them to contentment, convincing them that in any other walk of life they would be miserable.

Day after day, by ingenious and simple devices, they are given a horror of luxury, of all that appertains to the class above them. Pretty flowers and tempting chocolates are placed at the end of the nursery. The babies crawl towards them, fascinated. They touch the flowers and the chocolates. There is a sharp electric shock! The babies howl, and retreat. Every time they touch these pretty things, they are hurt. And so, gradually, they conceive a hatred for these things. They do not want them. Let the other class have them! This feeling remains with them for the rest of their lives. They are slaves, because they have been taught to *want* to be slaves.

Now I am going to ask you to apply this very simple and popular version of a scientific fact to the subject we are mainly concerned in discussing. Supposing that in your nursery there is a set of toy soldiers. There is a set in most nurseries all over the world. And supposing that every time your children touched them, they got an electric shock. It is really rather a funny idea, and I admit that it makes me emit faint gurgles of laughter even as I write it. So that we need not labour a point that is already obvious and might easily be made ridiculous.

What *is* ridiculous . . . and a good deal worse than ridiculous . . . is the idea of giving children toy soldiers at all. That is not at all funny, and it arouses in me not the smallest desire to laugh. A child's brain, as we have already observed, is of the most exquisite delicacy. Impressions received before the age of adolescence are printed on it for ever. They may be apparently forgotten, apparently overlaid, just as the bark of a grown tree may cover wounds which it received when it was a sapling. But underneath, in the subconscious, those impressions are as clear as ever, and for the rest of the child's life serve their purpose in modifying conduct and moulding ideas.

Just think, therefore, what you are doing when you put toy soldiers into the hands of a little boy. Soldiers . . . I imagine we will agree . . . are the emblems of war. The outward and visible sign of war. And these toy soldiers are pretty, brightly coloured, gay, amusing. So you are saying to the child 'War is pretty, and brightly coloured, too. It is happy. It is great fun. It is a game.

A *game!* It is the best game in the world. It is a much better game than education, for example. You can prove that merely by seeing how much brighter the soldiers are than the silly animals in your Noah's Ark. A much better game than art too, because you could certainly never find colours in your paint-box as brilliant as the red on your soldiers' tunics.'

You do not say these things, of course, in so many words, but you *are* saying them, implicitly, every minute of every hour that your son is stretched on the floor, ranging his little toys in their rows.

'Pop' go the guns! 'Bang, bang, bang' answers the enemy! A row of little figures falls over. The nursery fire flickers happily. It is charming, is it not? And yet, if you have any imagination, you may see strange things in the shadows cast by the fire-light. The little figures may not seem to stay quite still, as they fall, with a clink of metal, against each other. The limbs, perhaps, begin to twist and writhe, and the paint on the tunics begins to run. And surely . . . and here your heart gives an uncomfortable jump . . . surely there is a sort of mist spreading over the ground . . . a yellow mist . . . and when it touches the little figures, they writhe still more, in a way which would be very funny, if it did not remind you, somehow . . . of gas!

They told me, at the big stores round the corner, that the sale of toy soldiers had been larger this season than during any other season since the war. 'You see, sir,' said the salesman, holding up a model tank, 'we have so many attractive new models. There's always something novel, in fact, in this line of the toy business.'

VI

The seeds which you sow in the nursery do not take long to germinate. Any 'healthy' boy, by which we mean any boy who has absorbed the normal allowance of lunatic ideas from his parents, very soon shows a keen interest in all things military. He is taken to watch the changing of the guard at Whitehall. He is fascinated. *He* wants a tunic like that. *He* wants a lovely shiny breast-plate, and a helmet with plumes that the wind tosses wantonly. *He* wants to sit on a charger, while nursemaids, and other less excusable persons, slip notes into his beautiful great shiny boots!

You take him to the military tattoo at Aldershot. Oh — but it is beautiful, very beautiful and grand! He is growing up now, and his sense of the æsthetic is developing. For here, these long lines of men are as gay ribbons woven in an entrancing pattern, their swords are like silver fire, and their tunics are like red flowers. When the trumpet quivers through the night air, keen and true, it seems that no music could be sweeter. And is not the whole spectacle glorified, hazed over as with a flattering gauze, by the knowledge that all this beauty is also good and noble? That these men are heroes? That it is no mere ballet that is unfolding itself, but a pageant of bravery? England — my England! Your little boy may not say those words as he stumbles away, down the crowded steps, holding on to your hand. But he is thinking along those lines. Thinking passionately. Oh yes, you are making a good little soldier of him! You are making just the right material to be asphyxiated, shattered, drowned or otherwise destroyed, by some machine or other, in some country or other, as yet undecided.

Do you still intend to go on with the good work?

VII

Now, we can leave your small son, and concentrate on your own case.

Somewhere in your town, it is to be presumed, is a war memorial. It may not be a beautiful memorial, but every time you pass it, you feel a certain pride, a vague sense of glory. Perhaps it is because you knew some of the men whose names are carved on it. Or perhaps you are touched by the little bunches of flowers which are always laid on the steps. You wonder who put them there. You have never seen anybody putting any flowers on a war memorial. When do they do it? After dark, perhaps. Anyway, it is all very wonderful and very sad.

And yet, every time I pass one of these memorials I feel like crying out aloud. For to me they are no fitting monument to the glorious dead. They are, rather, a silent mockery, both of the dead and of the living.

There is not a single *true* war memorial in England. Nor in America, nor in France, nor in any country over which the storms have swept. For answer me this. What have these marble men, stretched beneath broken columns in quiet villages . . . what have they to do with war? These eagles, whose wings are so proud and arrogant above so many busy thoroughfares, how do they enter into it? These groups in bronze, these happy warriors, frozen on the march, a song on their lips, in a perpetual ecstasy, what *are* they? Why are they there? Who do they represent? What are they doing?

These emblems are cheating. *Cheating!* Because they have been hallowed by tears, no man would demand their destruction. But they should be removed to the peace of churchyards, where they belong, and taken away from the busy thoroughfares where fools may be corrupted by them. For all over the world these memorials tell the same lies. The words are in strange dialects. But it is the same story and the same marble soldier. And I believe that if those lips could speak, if a breath were to come through the cold stone, the same words would echo faintly . . . 'I died because they told me it was my duty. I died for my country. I was right. Wasn't I?'

And the appalling answer, the answer that tears the very soul of the man who makes it, is: 'No. You were wrong.'

Personally I see no reason why we should have war memorials at all. If the bubonic plague sweeps over a country, killing thousands of men, we do not erect shrines to it, as though it were something great and beautiful. War is doubly worse than plague, because it is infinitely more destructive and because it is deliberately chosen by man. Men do not inject themselves with the germs of plague, but they do inject themselves with the germs of war, and every war memorial is a fever spot, generating those germs.

If we cannot abolish those fever spots altogether, I should suggest that at least we sterilize them, by making them so hideous and so shocking that any war germs that might be lingering in the minds of children who played around them would be instantly killed. By the side of the plaques with the gilt lettering that hang up in the entrance halls of so many schools I would cause to be hung up a diagram of what a soldier's lungs look like after they have been eaten for a few hours by gas. I would reverently drape the statues, whether they were marching or sleeping, or waving flags or fixing bayonets, and I would build, in their place, little rooms to house volumes of photographs of the wounded. Only the strong of heart would be able to look at those photographs. I was once sent a volume of them by a German publisher. I did not know what I was going to see when I opened them. The indescribable horror and bestiality of those faces and bodies, pulped almost beyond recognition as human beings, is the most painful memory life holds for me. And those were just photographs!

If they could be published on this page there would be no need of any more words from me.

VIII

If war memorials are fever-spots, disseminating the germs of Mars, uniforms are even more dangerous as carriers of the fever. It is essential that you should realize the tremendous importance of the uniform as a war force. You will be falling into a grave error if you regard it as a mere harmless detail.

That importance will best be realized if you try to imagine war *without* uniform. Or if that is too much of an effort, try to imagine a war in which every soldier in every country wore the *same* uniform. Imagine that by some great international movement the armies of England, France, Germany, etc., had all adopted the same shade of cloth, the same cut, the same hat, the same buttons. (After all they were all, according to their leaders, fighting for the same things, for 'freedom', for 'justice', etc., so there was really no reason why they should put on different clothes to do it in.)

What would have happened in the last war, in such circumstances? Well obviously, the pitched battle would have been considerably less effective. Hand-to-hand encounters in no-man's-land would have been, to say the least of it, slowed up. If a company were scattered and disorganized, one platoon advanced, one platoon to the rear, and another platoon blown to pieces, and if the enemy were in a similar case, how would a man have known, in those dim and terrible hours of dawn, who was an enemy and who was a friend?

This idea of the universal uniform seemed so very simple when it first occurred to me that I immediately concluded there must be some 'snag' in it, and I took the trouble to inquire, from one or two men who had fought on the Western Front, if its results would have been as I suggested, in hand to hand fighting. 'Most certainly,' they said. 'It's obvious, isn't it? Very often, in a big push, you found yourself next in the line to some company of whom you didn't know a single man. And when things got in a hell of a mess, what *could* you do if there was absolutely nothing to distinguish one army from another? It'd be the same as though we'd all been naked.'

'However,' they added, 'I don't know if your idea

would be much use in these days, even if you could get it adopted. Because there'll probably be precious little hand to hand fighting in the next war.'

There I disagree. I am not thinking of the *practical* value of a universal uniform — which in actual war-time might quite well be nil. Even if the armies never saw each other, the commanders, in the various countries, would probably find it necessary to tie a coloured ribbon round their men's hats to distinguish them from the hated enemy. The idea may be of no value in time of war. But I believe it to be of real value in time of peace.

The uniform of the soldier is to war as the vestment of the priest to religion. The parallel between the military and the religious procedure is striking. To induce a war-like spirit the army has its military bands. To induce a military spirit the church has its anthems and its voluntaries. To cultivate the spirit of sacrifice, the army has its flags and its memorials, the church its coloured windows and its shrines. To ensure a strict discipline, the army has its standing orders and its drill, the church its prayer-book and its mass. To give the soldier an ideal he is told that if he lives and dies for his country he will be eternally glorious. To give the worshipper an ideal he is told that if he lives and dies for Christ he will be eternally glorious.

IX

Now let us go into your library.

It would be obviously impossible for me to pick out from your shelves all the books which glorify war. Nor do

I wish to do so. I would merely draw your attention to some of your books on the *last* war, and I would ask you to take these down, and study them again, in the light of what has gone before.

One book alone will serve as an example. It is Rupert Brooke's *1914 and Other Poems*. Over 140,000 copies of this volume have been sold. Extracts from it have been quoted on the graves of countless gallant young men. Sermons on it were preached by more than one bishop when I was at school. Its sonnets, of exquisite felicity, breathing the essence of a rare and fugitive spirit, have been lisped from mouth to mouth, have echoed in the strangest places, and go on echoing, with an ever falser note. The most famous sonnet of all need hardly be recalled to you. You know it by heart. . . .

If I should die, think only this of me
That there's some corner in a foreign land
That is for ever England. There shall be
In that rich earth, a richer dust concealed. . . .

Beautiful, is it not? The words, the rhythm, the sentiment . . . it is all so tranquil, so resigned. One pictures some fair youth sinking to rest in a quiet field . . . there is a red stain on his breast but the pain is soon gone . . . and he is asleep. And by some strange and lovely miracle his body mingles with the earth, and the poppies wave on the soil above him, keeping perpetual vigil.

Now, with that picture fresh in your mind, let me quote two quite casual sentences from Siegfried Sassoon's *Memoirs of an Infantry Officer*:

'*I particularly remember, as I passed down the trench,*

a pair of hands (nationality unknown), which protruded from the soaked ashen soil like the roots of a tree turned upside down. And floating on the surface of the flooded trench was the mask of a human face which had detached itself from the skull.'

Which of those pictures struck you most? Rupert Brooke's or Siegfried Sassoon's? Which do you prefer . . . the poetry or the prose? The painted allegory or the stark snapshot? The soothing legend or the revolting truth?

It is for you to choose. And as you choose, so you must act. If you do not wish the 'mask' of your own son's face . . . 'detached from its skull' . . . to go floating down some drain as yet undug, then you should not send him to schools where the masters encourage these things by reading such poems to impressionable youths . . . poems which make a soldier's death sound much finer, and much less painful, than scoring a try in a football game.

They ban Russian literature. They ban scientific essays on sexual phenomena . . . essays which should be propped up under the nose of every English judge. They ban the passionate, bleeding prose of D. H. Lawrence. Yet they distribute Rupert Brooke wholesale.

Well, either 'they' are mad, or I am. And I am not afraid of the verdict of posterity.

X

But after all, it is not the books that *you* are reading which matter so much. Your son's books are much more important. So let us pay him a visit at his school. You will, I am sure, excuse me for asking you to make this little excursion. The request is due to a suspicion that though you may be fairly well aware of what they are doing to your son's body, you may not be quite so well acquainted with their efforts to influence his mind.

It is really worth our while to make this effort. For, after all, he *is* your son, and really, you love him more than anything else in the world. You aren't particularly religious — you certainly don't pray with any sort of regularity — but you do sometimes pray for him, a little self-consciously, a little secretively, that he will grow up strong and healthy and clean, and play a worthy part in the battle of life. Yes, and an intelligent part, too, because, damn it all, life's more difficult than it was when you were a boy. A man has to have his wits about him. Life's a struggle all right, nowadays.

Very well, let us see how you are equipping him for that struggle.

Let us look over his shoulder as he works. It is a hot summer morning — eleven o'clock on a hot Saturday morning — and the history lesson is just beginning. He's reading something — what is it? He'll be examined on it soon, so we might as well see. Ah! *The Political History of England, 1485 to 1547*. By H. A. L. Fisher. Damned good chap Fisher. Wasn't he Minister of Education, or something? That's the stuff to give the troops. That's the sort of thing your boy *ought* to learn . . . with all this unrest, and these trade unions, and unemployed, and what not. Let's see what he's reading. . . .

'*On September 7th*, 1513, *Surrey lay at Wooler Haugh, about six miles to the south-east of Flodden crest.*'

Did he, now? You never knew that before, did you? No! Very interesting. Most instructive. Let's get on.

'*To attack the Scots in their strong position would have been folly, and on the 8th Surrey recrossed the Till and marched to Barmoor, six miles due east of the Scottish camp.*'

Quite. Across the Till. To Barmoor. Obviously the right thing to do. Very important. You try to get a look at your son's face to see if he is taking this all in. But somehow you can't see it very clearly. Never mind, the printed page is clear enough, and on it you read:

'*Once encamped at Barmoor, the English army was sheltered from observation by a low range of hills; and here Surrey took a momentous decision.*'

A momentous decision! My word, now, this is interesting. Momentous, says Mr. Fisher! You feel you are really in the heart of things. Let us read on:

'*The vanguard, under the admiral,* 9,000 *strong and accompanied by the guns, moved due north, and recrossing the Till at Twizel Bridge placed itself across James's communications. The rest of the army under Surrey crossed higher up the river by Millford and Sandyford, and . . .*'

Here, wait a minute. Let's get this straight. Where are they now? They've gone back across the Till again? Why did they want to do that, just when you'd learned that bit? And they went over *Twizel* bridge, did they? Twizel — that's a fool name. Could it be a misprint? No . . . there it is, as large as life, Twizel . . . and you're sure it's awfully important to remember.

But it is difficult, isn't it? Because, you see, it's so very hot in the class-room. And outside, far away in the high blue air, an aeroplane's droning, on and on, like a tiresome fly. And still further away you remember that there are cities in distress, in the grip of strange unrest . . . an unrest which you don't quite understand, with which you vaguely sympathize, though you deplore the fact that your dividends aren't coming in as they used to.

We will therefore leave Mr. Fisher, and turn to the principal history book which is used to-day for the average boy in the average public school.

XI

It is called *The Groundwork of British History* and it is written by Mr. George Townsend Warner, sometime Fellow of Jesus College, Cambridge, and Mr. C. H. K. Marten, of Balliol College, Oxford. Thousands of English schoolboys' knowledge of the world in general was gathered from the pages of this book. Or would it be more accurate to say that it enshrines the ignorance of the younger generation?

Let us judge for ourselves. Let us ask ourselves the question 'Who are the men, in the history of the British Empire, who will be reckoned to have played a decisive part in these whirling years?' We need not be too 'modern', because the book was last issued in the year 1929. We can merely confine ourselves to the first ten years after the war.

Well, obviously, one of the most important men in the recent history of the British Empire is Gandhi. We look him up in the index. Odd! He is not mentioned! In the G's, where he should be, there is quite a lot about the Gesiths, who were a band of disagreeable savages in the employment of the kings of Wessex long before the Norman Conquest. There is also a lot about the author of the *Decline and Fall of the Roman Empire.* But there is nothing whatever about the man who, according to our elders and betters in the press, may yet be the author of the Decline and Fall of another Empire.

Let us try somebody else. Who, according to the popular press, has been one of the greatest enemies that the British Empire has ever known? Who was going to ruin us all? To bring our institutions crumbling to the ground? To fetter us, starve us, torture us? Lenin – was it not? We look him up in the index. We draw another blank. Under the L's, where this monster should have been pinned down for our edification, we find only the Earl of Leicester, who did a number of supremely unimportant things in the middle of the thirteenth century. And under him is the Duke of Leinster, quite a modern young man, for he commanded the Dublin contingent against a French invasion during the war of American Independence. With what results, we are not informed. He has just been dragged in, presumably, because he was a Duke.

We are beginning to be puzzled. The index seems to contain more blanks than prizes. We had better choose somebody absolutely safe, if we are not going to be disappointed again, somebody of quite unchallengeable importance, long before the year 1929, long before the war, even. Somebody like Ramsay MacDonald.

We look him up, and we find Flora Macdonald, page

486. Above her is Macbeth, King of Scotland, page 133. Below her are the Macdonalds of Glencoe, page 457. Of Ramsay there is not even the faintest hint.

This is getting desperate. Who *is* of importance, in the eyes of Messrs. Warner and Marten? What about Mr. de Valera? We look him up. Not a word! Well — if they think it more discreet not to mention the enemies of the Empire, what about the Empire's servants? Haig, for example? Not a word!

Perhaps they are ardent feminists, then? Perhaps we have been studying the index from the wrong angle? Let us look up Christabel Pankhurst. She may be regarded, surely, as a person of some importance? What do we find? We find the surrender of Pampeluna. Just that, and nothing more.

Do you want your boy to learn about the surrender of Pampeluna? Do you think it will help him, in this year of grace? It really is important that you should answer this question, and answer it honestly. It is of no use to put me off with vague generalizations about 'getting a broad view of history', or about 'studying the past in order to be able to weigh the future in the balance'. I want you to answer the question 'Do you want your boy to learn about the surrender of Pampeluna?'

It will be easy for the professional historian, who is usually a master of equivocation to pour scorn on these jejune queries, just as it was always easy for the professional theologians to pour scorn on the first scientists. This does not worry me at all. Because, whenever I feel there is a danger of losing the argument, I shall just protrude my lips and lisp, in childish tones, 'Do you wish your boy to learn about the surrender of Pampeluna?' For you see, something primitive, and probably unpleasant, inside me, tells me that there is no answer to that question.

XII

However, since the above section contains enough material to make any old-fashioned headmaster foam at the mouth with rage, and since it is written in a style obviously calculated to irritate, let us cease this banter for a moment, and look at the matter from another point of view.

I want you, in this discussion of history, to consider a biological parallel which seems to me of considerable significance.

We are not certain how life began on this earth, but we *are* certain that it was a very lengthy and hesitant business. The strange miracles that were born among the Proterozoic rocks were no sudden flashes of sudden life-creation, no swift stirring of fins or lungs along the steamy shores of the primeval world. It was all incredibly tedious and illimitably wasteful.

We need not speculate on the probable length of the vast æons of the Proterozoic Age, the Palæozoic Age, the Mesozoic Age, etc. etc. We need not examine the odd structure of the Cotylosaur, nor chronicle the first appearance of fur and feathers. We have only to note the almost unimaginable *time* that was needed to effect any change in the structure of animal life — the millions and millions of years which were required for the odd evolutions of the first bird-like creatures, for example. Over immense periods they hopped. Over equally immense periods they skimmed. It was not till the world was already old that they flew, with clumsy creaking wings, over the dark forests.

Millions of years to change the colour of a feather! Millions of years to put an inch on to the fourth finger of the Pterodactyl! Millions of years to push out the long jaws of the Tetrabelodon! And how many millions to produce any creature even vaguely resembling a man!

Now, here is the point. Supposing, in the biological evolution of the world's species we were told that for one hundred million years life had been emerging from the stage of the jelly-fish. 100,000,000 years. And then, supposing we were told that in the space of only fifty years, the jelly-fish made a tremendous and swift advance in structure and in intelligence. That there was a sudden miraculous stirring. That the jelly-fish developed out of all knowledge. Split up into groups. Grew legs, eyes, wings. That from them, in this flash of time, the whole modern animal kingdom, with its infinite diversity of life, was born. All in fifty years!

Supposing that were the case, would we not consider it necessary to study those last fifty years at least as fully as the preceding 100,000,000 years? Would we not consider the period, in which these vital and revolutionary changes occurred, to be at least as important as the 100,000,000 years which preceded it? Or would we be blinded by the mere *length* of the first period — would we go on studying jelly-fish after jelly-fish, with painful monotony, merely adding a footnote at the end of our book to say that a great number of interesting things had happened between the years 100,000,000 and 100,000,050, but that they really need not concern us?

XIII

Is not this what we are doing in our teaching of modern history? Is the parallel really so far fetched?

In the last fifty years man, the animal, has changed quite as completely and as radically as my imaginary jelly-fish. He has grown wings, ears, eyes, new legs, new arms. He can fly in the air, swim under the sea, race across the land. He has, in addition, an entirely new set of senses. And he is still developing so rapidly that God alone knows what he may not become before the century is out.

Now, do you see my point? Now, do you see why it is criminal folly to teach history as we are teaching it? And now, do you feel that you can answer, with a certain amount of assurance, the question, 'Do you want your son to spend his days learning about the surrender of Pampeluna?'

All this has a very direct bearing on the subject of war and peace. In the first chapter of this book I suggested that 'until August, 1914, the word "war" meant to the nations of the world what it had always meant, since the days of Napoleon . . . indeed, since the days of Hannibal.' It was 218 years before the birth of Christ when Hannibal marched south through Gaul and crossed the Alps. A good deal over two thousand years elapsed between that brilliantly futile exploit and the outbreak of the Great War. But though the beginning of the Next Great War will be, in all probability, less than twenty years since the beginning of the Last Great War, those twenty years have brought changes far stranger and more radical than the two thousand years which went before.

It is really vital that the teachers of our sons should realize this. I feel convinced that they do *not* realize it. If they did, they would throw up their hands in horror at the cruel and tragic way in which they are misleading youth. Day in and day out they are teaching them about these little wars of the past — these pretty, tiny affairs of flags and streamers, these manœuvres as agreeable as the movements of an old-fashioned dance. And always these phenomena are given the name of 'war', so that when a boy thinks of the next 'war', he thinks in terms of his history books. This is a very terrible error, for which all parents are directly responsible. The next war will bear no more resemblance to the last than the trilobite to the sabre-toothed tiger. The march of science has accelerated a million-fold. To fail to tell boys this is as criminally neglectful as to fail to tell a child that it will be burnt if it plays with living coals.

Now do you still want your son to spend his days learning about the surrender of Pampeluna?

XIV

If you have read so far you will have read far enough to fall into a grave error regarding the educational theories which I am advocating. It is quite possible that you may be saying to yourself 'So we are to be utterly "modern" are we? To scrap the history books for the newspapers? To ignore the tremendous lessons which history has to offer us by its contemplation of the lives and struggles and characters of men? To regard our social institutions as mushroom growths, whose early struggles are of no interest? What rot! Such theories would produce, in a few generations, a race of half-baked, loose-thinking, irresponsible vulgarians.'

I quite agree. Such theories would. I have never advocated them and never shall. All I am suggesting is a change of *emphasis*. The modern history book devotes one paragraph to Newton and ten pages to the Duke of Wellington. I suggest that the ten pages should be given to Newton and the paragraph to Wellington. (He is not worth more than a footnote, but we must not do these things too violently.) Nor are these anachronisms evident only when war is in question. The modern history book devotes a paragraph to the growth of the Trade Unions and a whole chapter to the Elizabethan ecclesiastical settlement. It seems to me that this procedure should be exactly reversed. The intelligent modern schoolboy could write you quite a good essay on the history of artillery but he would make a very feeble showing if he were to attempt to trace the history of architecture. One could develop this point *ad infinitum*. Our history books are merely long and wearisome monotones on the things which have died or the things which have caused death. The living and the creative, the healers, the liberators, the deathless army of inventors, of poets, and of martyrs — these are given a back place in the pageant. You cannot see the landscape because of the flags. You cannot hear the march of humanity because of the beating of the drums. You cannot see the new civilization because of the monuments and the memorials, blocking out the view.

I said this was going to be a long chapter. It has already out-run its appointed space. There is no point in going on.

However, if a single reader has been convinced, it will not have been written in vain. For this revolution in international thought, which I am advocating, has got to begin with one man in one nation. And perhaps that man may be you.

CHAPTER XV

LETTER TO A YOUNG MAN

DEAR JOHN,

You have written to me telling me that your father is returning home next week, after a year in the Colonies, and that he is 'utterly furious' with you because he has heard that at Oxford you voted for the famous Union resolution . . . 'That this house will in no circumstances fight for King and Country.'

You quote him as saying, 'if that is the sort of thing they teach you at Oxford, you had better leave, cut your schools, and go straight out to British East Africa, to get some sense knocked into your head.' You are naturally worried by this ultimatum. You are very fond of your father. You are also very fond of Oxford, and I gather that you have every chance of taking a first in 'greats' at the end of next term. At the same time, you were really serious when you recorded that vote. It was not merely a frivolous gesture. 'I feel this whole thing too deeply to be stampeded into denying it,' you write to me. And you add, 'But I terribly want moral support. You know what my family is . . . how conventional they all are . . . how they set at one until one feels inclined to scream.' You finish up with an urgent request that I should send you 'a sort of pocket speech for the defence which any young son who believes in peace at any price can learn by heart, and produce on all occasions, when his parents are getting him down.'

Well, I don't know if I can do exactly that. If you have read this book, you will realize that though, in theory, I am for peace at any price, I am not absolutely certain whether the theory will work. However, I must not begin on a negative note. There is no need. There are too many positive things your father must learn, in his own interests.

Firstly, about this motion. Extreme pacifist as I am, if I had been President, I should not have brought forward such a motion. I consider it offensive to a man who is rightly beloved by the English people . . . a man who has himself done great work for peace. I should have phrased it:

> 'That this House will not fight for any Ruler or any Country.'

This motion would have been just as effective and would not have so outraged public taste.

How would I have voted? I don't know. I have at last come to the conclusion that in certain circumstances I would fight in an international army, in an international cause, under some commander appointed by the League of Nations. This sounds extremely funny, and if your friends in the Tory Club get to hear of it, they will be able to write delicious parodies about it. Lovely squibs and verses about me, forming fours in Geneva, and being told to 'dress by the left,' in bad French. Oh yes . . . I am handing them a rich gift of satire. They will not use it nearly so amusingly as I should use it myself, nor will they exploit its heaven-sent comedy so delicately. Still, they will do very well. It is a fool-proof idea, for anybody with a sense of satire.

However, we are not worrying any longer about my case, but about yours. You want to be able to defend that vote when your father returns. And you should have the courage to tell him, that though the motion was offensive, the meaning behind it was desperately sincere. For the young men know, only too well, how that phrase 'King and Country' is abused by the politicians. Your 'King and Country' may be in danger, certainly, but they may be in danger simply because of the folly of your country's ministers, or the aggressiveness of your country's policy. If you are going to abrogate your right to criticize those ministers and that policy, and also to deny the right of other nations to criticize it, you land yourself in the lunatic and criminal position of the man who says 'my country, right or wrong'. Which is as though a man were to say 'my sister, mad or sane, my brother, murderer or innocent'. Just because a girl is your sister you do not claim the *right* to allow her to walk the streets as a homicidal lunatic. Just because a man is your brother you do not claim the *right* to assault those policemen who arrest him for murder. You do not do these things because you realize you are a social being, subject to certain laws which men have made for their own protection. You do not do these things because you believe in law as opposed to anarchy.

Therefore, you must ask your father this question (which I have asked earlier in my book), 'Do you believe in anarchy or do you believe in law?' And when he has told you that he believes in law, you must point out to him that the phrase 'King and Country' is, often, a deliberate flouting of the law of nations. It is tantamount to a declaration of absolute sovereignty.

II

However, I realize only too well that when your father comes home, when his trunks have been carried upstairs, and the souvenirs produced, when you are eventually summoned to his study for this dreadful cross-examination, he will be little inclined to reason. He will drag out all the old questions, and you must be prepared to answer them. And I will wager ten to one that almost the first question he asks you will be:

'What would you do if you found a great hulking German attacking your sister? Wouldn't you fight *then*?'

This is the militarist's standard question. Having asked it, your father will lean back in his chair and survey you almost amiably, because, you see, he thinks there is no answer to the question. He thinks he's got you now, poor misguided lad that you are! And it would be ungentlemanly of him to exult too obviously in his intellectual triumph.

He is pitifully wrong, of course. There is not only an answer to this question . . . there are a great many answers, and you can vary them according to the temperament of the questioner. The quickest and most effective reply is, 'I should behave exactly in the same way as if I found a great hulking Britisher attacking my sister — i.e. I should give him a sock in the jaw.'

As soon as you introduce this parallel, your father's

argument becomes ridiculous. By giving the imaginary assailant of your sister a sock in the jaw you are merely temporarily taking the part of the police. The army and the police have entirely different functions — one exists to break the law, the other to keep it.

However, the true argument of course goes a good deal deeper than that. It goes as deep as Christianity itself, though it might embarrass your father if you were to use that word, which does not sound quite 'nice', out of Church. The true argument is that if you wish to avoid the possibility of large numbers of women, of every nationality, being outraged, you must avoid war, at almost any cost. You will not drive out passion by passion. Soldiers are much alike, whatever uniform they may wear. But when they are in enemy territory, when they are doped with lies which make them believe that every German is a devil and that every German nurse tortures the wounded (or vice versa, because the German stories about English nurses were exactly the same as ours), then you induce a state of mind which makes these soldiers feel that no treatment to which they could submit such she-devils could be too vile.

You might also tell your father that this question about your sister is not only unintelligent, but cowardly. *It is hitting below the belt.* It is trying to trap you on a false analogy. It is confusing a vitally personal issue, which offers only one judgment and one method of treatment, with an entirely impersonal issue, which is open to many judgments and many methods of treatment. For what conceivable connection can be drawn between the blow which you deliver, in hot blood, against a man who is doing your family a great wrong, and the shot you fire, in cold blood, into the dark, in the hope that it may split the skull of some man you have never seen, some puzzled chap who, if the diplomatic wheel had spun another turn, might be your friend?

Learn that last question by heart. And when you say it to your father, ask him if he can deny that his own question was confused, unjust and a perfect example, as I said, of hitting below the belt.

III

As the argument with your father quickens, he will probably ask you — 'But don't you think that *any* cause can be just? Is there nothing you would fight for?'

Now, of course, on this point you and I differ. You say that there is *nothing* for which you would fight. I say that I would probably fight in an international army for an international cause. Yours is the nobler, more logical attitude, but it may get you into worse hot water than mine. However, I can help you in your argument.

Listen. You will begin, of course, by pointing out to your father that the 'justice' or 'injustice' of the cause has nothing whatever to do with the case. War does not settle who was right or wrong. It settles who was strongest. This is so childishly evident that I apologize for suggesting that your father needs to be told it.

What I am getting at is this. Sooner or later, in your argument, your father is bound to pin you down to the policy you tell me most of you really voted for, in that Oxford resolution, the policy of *passive resistance*. You are one of a large number of intelligent and representative young Englishmen who have deliberately chosen this as their programme in the event of war. Mind you, I don't go with you all the way — I don't believe the theory is workable. You do. And since you do, I implore you to make the *best* of your case. Most of you seem to do your utmost to make the worst of it. You are flummoxed by your cross-examiners, who draw pictures of a nation in chains, a countryside laid waste, etc. etc. You know, as well as I do, that these pictures are silly little bogy pictures, which are not worthy of the serious consideration of an intelligent scullery-maid, but you do not seem able to convince your persecutors of this fact.

Therefore, read these last few pages very slowly and carefully please.

IV

Your case for passive resistance can be proved in one way and one only, by imagining it put into practice, in some specific instance, and by pinning your opponent down to the definite losses and injuries which, in his opinion, we should suffer, and by making him prove that these losses and injuries are likely to be greater than the losses and injuries we suffered in the last war. He must therefore prove that passive resistance would cost this country more than £9,590,000,000 and nearly 700,000 men killed, and more, morally, than is witnessed by the sense of utter futility and rottenness which broods over all our younger generation. These are the things that he must prove. And in order to prove them he must stick to facts.

Here are the facts:

In the old days a conquered nation paid for its helplessness by four forms of tribute — by money, by services, by land, and by the surrender of various forms of booty which are best described as miscellaneous.

Let us see if and how these forms of tribute could be exacted from England, on the assumption that England was completely non-resistant . . . that we simply threw up our hands and said, 'all right, come on, take what you want.'

Firstly, money. We are constantly being assured by all the big capitalists, especially the press lords, that the British people have reached the limit of taxation, and that further imposts will bring the whole of our financial edifice tumbling to the ground. We are also assured that the foundation of that edifice is the subtle cement called 'credit', which is more important in determining the value of the pound sterling than all the gold in the Bank of England. The pound sterling, too, as we are so often reminded, is an international currency. One third of the world is 'on' sterling. So that any severe shock to sterling reacts to the detriment of the whole economic structure of the world.

In the light of these facts, you might therefore ask your father what, exactly, a conquering nation will *do*, in this question of taking our money. Seize the gold in the Bank, for example? There is no statesman in the silliest party of the silliest country in Europe who would any longer advocate such a folly, after the experience of the last few years. Nations now know, only too well, that a surplus of gold is only an encumbrance. We have just seen the ludicrous paradox whereby the richest citizen in the richest country in the world was unable to draw a single cent from his bank, gorged as it was with gold. (I refer, of course, to the banking crisis which broke on the day of President Roosevelt's inauguration.) So we are not likely to see any nation taking away our gold, even if we open the vaults for them.

How else, then, are they to take our money? In stocks and shares? But these are only of value as long as our credit is good. Take away our credit and they are so much paper.

By doubling our taxes, then? But the economists and the press lords tell us that we *can't* be taxed any more. It would send sterling down to zero. The international reactions would be appalling. Every country's currency would stagger. Who is going to risk that? The sturdy Germans? The canny French? The disciplined Italians? The hard-hit Americans? The ultra-Tory Japanese? The tortured Central Europeans? Well? *Who* wants sterling to go to damnation?

If your father can answer these questions, he will either be an exceptionally able or an exceptionally stupid man.

Now we come to the second form of tribute — services. 'We should be turned into a nation of slaves' we are informed. Very well. How? Where? When? In what way are we going to set to work for our conquerors? Remember, they have millions of unemployed of their own. It is hardly likely that out of mere spite they will employ Britons to engage in vast industrial or agricultural schemes when their own countrymen are chafing at their own idleness.

Now do you see how silly the militarist is in *that* section of his argument, at least? He throws up his hands in horror at the thought of the English people being forced to work by their conquerors. And, in the next breath, he deplores the enforced idleness of three million of his fellow-countrymen. He really cannot have it both ways.

This second section is linked to the first by the overlapping of 'services' and 'goods'. Your father's suggestion implies that the people of England will all be set to sewing and stitching and digging and riveting in order that the people of some other nation may benefit by their activities. However, all you have to do, to settle him there, is to ask him why nations which erect prohibitive tariffs round their frontiers, in order to keep our goods *out*, when they are at peace with us, should suddenly abolish those tariffs in order to let our goods *in* . . . just because they have defeated us. Well? Why?

We therefore come to the third form of tribute which might be exacted — land. I imagine that your father will not be so misguided as to suggest that any nation in its senses particularly wishes to 'annex' Kent or Suffolk or Yorkshire. What conceivable object could they have in doing so? Supposing that France, for example, decided that she would like a strip of the South Coast. Well? What effect would that have . . . apart from the fact that the French would presumably have little use for the laws which make Englishmen criminals if they have a drink after ten o'clock? If you are feeling frivolous you might mention this fact to your father when he is playing an obligato on the theme of 'Britons never will be slaves'.

But you are not feeling frivolous. You want to get this question of tribute by land settled, and therefore you must obviously face the problem of the annexation of the colonies. You must be prepared to say 'all right — let 'em take the colonies'. And having said that, I expect your father will lose his patience, and show you the door.

However, if, in the process of saying good-bye, you have an opportunity of asking him a few further questions, you might require him to be a little more particular as to who is to 'take' what. It might be rather a large problem, for example, to 'take' Canada. The only nation who would be wishful to 'take' it would be America and one may reasonably ask what advantages America would gain thereby which she does not enjoy already. America and Canada form a geographical and economic unit. Along the vast frontier no single fort has been built, no single gun ever fires. How does America 'take' Canada, except by lowering tariffs? And this object the respective nations are working for at this moment, for their mutual benefit!

Or is Australia in question? Perhaps your father has never been to Australia? I have. And in spite of the endlessly reiterated arguments in favour of a 'white' Australia, I was struck by the monstrous injustice of the dog-in-the manger policy which keeps a continent larger than Europe as the special perquisite of six million people who do not know how to manage it. There are more people in the City of London than in the whole of this vast area. If you go across Australia in a train you will see, as you pass through New South Wales, mile upon mile of orchard-land where the fruit rots on the ground because there is nobody to pick it up.

Yet, if you stay in Melbourne, you will find that about the only restaurant where you can get a decent meal at a reasonable price is run by an Italian who has somehow or other evaded the immigration laws. And if you send your shirt to be washed in Sydney you will be wise to choose a Chinese laundry.

Australia is a glorious country. The young men there are like gods, running in the sunshine. The young women are incredibly vital and radiant (and irritating). And the politicians, with their 'White Australia' policy are enough to make the mildest man blaspheme.

We are off the rails again. But you might make your father look at the map, before he turns you out of the house, and learn a few statistics.

There remains, as a major problem in this land question, Africa. I do not know enough about this to discuss it. You must look this up for yourself. You had better concentrate on Kenya Colony. It seems to be a part of the map which we have coloured quite a bright red, in view of the matrimonial eccentricities of those who frequent it.

Lastly, booty. We are back again in our damnably frivolous mood, and the nature of this section is not going to help us to escape it. For if your father draws for you a lurid picture of a band of alien savages marching into the National Gallery, all you have to do is to ask him when he last went to the National Gallery. Quite a long time ago, wasn't it? And what did he see there? Which masterpiece most impressed him? Oh yes — you know all about Sargent's picture of Lord Ribblesdale, but that was in all the illustrated annuals last Christmas. Apart from

Sargent's picture of Lord Ribblesdale, what is the name of the masterpiece that he, personally, would most miss?

I apologize for these light excusions. You see, I keep on visualizing your father's face before me . . . red and angry, and at the same time, afraid. I am trying so hard to find out what he is afraid of. I don't seem to be succeeding very well, and I suppose the disappointment causes a nervous reaction which forces a wild flippancy upon me, when I would be serious.

At least, however, I hope you will agree that I may have strengthened the somewhat hazy arguments for passive resistance which you had previously advanced to me.

V

And now, I'm almost through and the little jokes with which I have tried to enliven this utterly bitter subject no longer come to my pen. Because I am thinking of your brother, and how he was killed in that filthy way, on his first day, only 48 hours before the Armistice. Your father will be thinking of him too, during all this long and agonizing conversation — and so will you, I expect, though you were only a kid when he died. And your father may be comparing you two, in his mind, wondering how one son could be so fine and the other so contemptible. Yes — you might as well realize that's what he'll be thinking.

What must you do?

You must walk up to him, and you must speak very quietly and calmly. You must say to him:

'Ted died for me. You told him, and everybody else

told him, that he was fighting in a war to end war. *To end war.* That was really what he died for. He didn't die for the mess we're in now. He didn't die in order that we should all be at each others' throats again, before the willow tree you planted on his grave had time to grow tall enough to throw its shadow.

'Please, father, don't hate me for reminding you of that. Ted wouldn't have hated me for it. Ted wasn't the hating sort. He just did what he thought was his duty. I believe I'm doing mine now, in the same way. It isn't as hard for me as it was for him, God knows. But it isn't easy, either. I do beg of you to believe me when I say that.

'Ted would have believed me. He might even have agreed with me. For do you think that he could rest happily if he were able to see me putting on the same old uniform, listening to the same old lies, marching to the same old tunes . . . *to remind him that he died in vain?* For if I have to go through it all again, did he not die in vain? Please, father, you must answer that. And if you answer it wrongly. I'm done. Just done.'

VI

And now, my friend, I am done too. I don't know if this letter has been any help to you. I only know that the writing of it has been a help to me, in making me realize my deathless kinship with my brother man, and my love for him, beside which no hate can flourish.

BEVERLEY NICHOLS